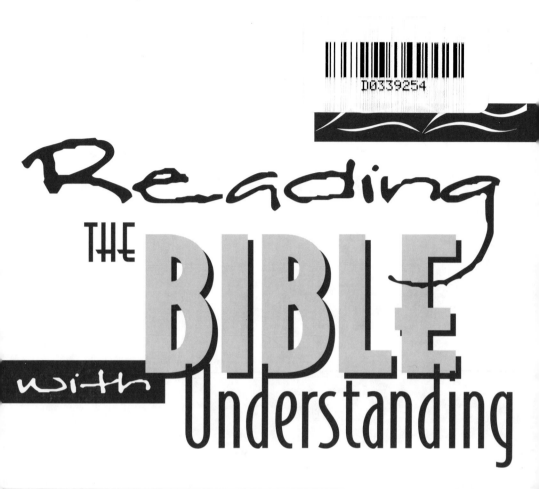

# Reading
## THE
# BIBLE
## with
## Understanding

## BY LANE A. BURGLAND

**CPH**

Edited by Arnold E. Schmidt

# Contents

# Introduction

Talking … listening … writing … reading. Each requires a unique set of skills. When we personally listen to someone who is speaking, we receive all sorts of clues to help us figure out what the other person means. Speakers use gestures, tone of voice, and rate of delivery to communicate their message. We see body language and hear changes in a person's delivery.

The process for writing and reading is different. We see and hear none of these clues when we read what someone has written. Therefore a writer must use care and planning when putting thoughts down on paper in order to communicate the intended meaning. A reader, too, carefully reads and reflects on a text to interpret and understand what an author means.

In a way, reading the Bible is like reading any other book (or collection of books). A person reads a series of words that make up sentences and paragraphs and seeks to comprehend what is read. As literature or as history, the Bible is an open book. Anyone can read what is written (assuming it is translated well enough) and get the facts of the story—who did what to whom, where and when it occurred. The difficulty comes when we ask, "So what does it mean?"

Sometimes we hear people say that one person's interpretation is just as good as another's, or that any individual's understanding of a Bible passage is valid for that person. Our own experience should tell us that this is not true. When we write a letter to someone, we have a purpose in writing and want our reader to understand what we say. We write as clearly as possible, choosing the right words for our purpose, so that our reader doesn't misunderstand us.

God does the same thing with the Bible. Over a period of many centuries, through a variety of human authors, God has communicated His message. He wants us to understand both the facts of the story and His purpose in writing. (See John 20:30–31.) Reading the Bible with understanding means that we do not merely seek to understand the history of God's people or the story line of great literature. We read the Bible to understand what God says to us. We ask, "What does this mean?" and "What does this mean to me?" At this point the Holy Spirit's guidance is essential.

Our own sinful nature blinds us to the Good News of Jesus Christ. (See Paul's comments in 2 Corinthians 4:3–4.) Reading the Bible is thus a spiritual battle and not only an intellectual exercise.

The story of a blind man in John 9 parallels our reading of the Bible. Jesus healed that blind man. Later, when Jesus revealed Himself to that man, the formerly blind man saw His Savior and His Lord. He believed in Jesus and worshiped Him (John 9:38). The Pharisees saw the same Jesus as did the blind man. Yet, in unbelief, they saw Jesus as an enemy of God and the Law. Both the formerly blind man and the Pharisees looked at the same Man, but they came away with vastly different understandings. Were both "interpretations" of Jesus valid? Not at all! The blind man came away with true spiritual sight, the forgiveness of sins, and salvation. The Pharisees went away spiritually blind, condemned in their sin (John 9:41). The eternal destiny of all of these people rested on whether or not they understood who Jesus is—Son of God and Savior of the world.

In a similar way, what do people see when they read the Bible? Do they see a historical book of literature, or do they see the living Word of God (Hebrews 4:12)? As previously stated, reading the Bible does have much in common with reading any other book or letter. Its meaning is plain to anyone who reads it with an open mind. At the same time, reading the Bible is a unique experience; the Holy Spirit shows us our Savior in it.

Reading the Bible is not only an intellectual exercise; it is primarily the pursuit of the person who knows Jesus Christ as Savior and Lord and who wants to be "complete, thoroughly equipped for every good work" (as Paul says of Scripture in 2 Timothy 3:17).

When we pick up the Bible, we should be honest with ourselves. We already have some ideas about what the Bible is all about and how to go about reading it. Everybody does. These become the principles we follow when we interpret the Bible.

In part 1 we will examine five principles of interpretation and illustrate how they work for us. These rules are based on claims the Bible makes about itself, and they are confirmed by our own experiences as we read what other people write to us. The principles have been developed over the years to help us grasp what the author(s) meant. In part 1 we also will discuss the distinction between Law and Gospel, a critical tool for reading the Bible.

Part 2 will concentrate on more difficult passages in the Bible. We will examine literary categories such as poetry, prophecy, parables, and apocalyptic writing (such as Revelation). Study of some passages will require the use of Bible dictionaries and encyclopedias. You will receive some "hands-on" experience with those tools.

Finally, in part 3 we will give you some information about the Bible: who wrote the various books, when they were written, how we got our English Bible, and a quick evaluation of various Bible translations and paraphrases.

A number of good translations are available. The New American Standard (NAS), New Revised Standard Version (NRSV), the New King James Version (NKJV), and the New International Version (NIV) are all popular. We will trace the history of these translations in chapter 15. For the purposes of this course, we will use the Concordia Self-Study Bible (CSSB), which contains the New International Version.

Since the Bible is a collection of 66 books, finding your way around in it can be somewhat of a challenge. Use your table of contents as a resource and a guide. Some people can look up passages by book, chapter, and verse very quickly. They have spent years acquiring that skill, so don't become discouraged if it takes you a while to find a particular section of the Bible.

May God bless you as you begin your study of His Word!

Lane A. Burgland
Churubusco, Indiana

# Part One

## Principles of Interpretation

The Bible was written many centuries ago in a setting far different from our own. Therefore a student of the Bible might ask, "How can I understand what the Bible is saying? The people, the cultures, and the language are from a different age, and I am living in a modern age. Furthermore, I am not a theologian. I haven't gone to a seminary. Who will explain the meaning of the Bible to me?"

This seeming barrier is really no barrier at all. With the aid of the Holy Spirit, the student discovers that certain "keys" can help one understand the Bible and apply its timeless truths. These keys, known also as principles of interpretation, are contained within the Bible itself. Thus, the Bible presents itself as an open book, with treasured meanings that can be understood by any Christian serious enough to seek God's message of salvation.

The principles in this text fall under the umbrella of three overriding beliefs:

• Scripture alone is the authority, not human reason.

• We are saved only by God's grace (His undeserved love).

• We receive God's grace only through faith in Jesus Christ.

The more we read the Bible, the clearer it becomes that these three beliefs are drawn from Scripture itself.

# Stick with the Plain and Obvious Meaning of a Text

## Defining the Principle

Communication is a difficult art. We choose our words and we put them together in sentences, hoping the other person will understand what we are saying or writing. At times, though, we don't say what we mean or mean what we say. Sometimes we use irony or sarcasm to make our point, sometimes we exaggerate or use hyperbole for emphasis, and sometimes we use puns and wordplays for humorous effect.

The best rule of thumb when reading Scripture is to read it as straightforward communication unless the text contains some indicator that we should disregard the usual and customary meaning of the words or paragraphs.

> THE FIRST PRINCIPLE IS TO TAKE THE WORDS OF SCRIPTURE IN THE NORMAL, INTENDED SENSE UNLESS THE CONTEXT COMPELS US TO UNDERSTAND THE WORDS IN SOME OTHER WAY.

## Applying the Principle

### Mark 5:21–43

Perhaps the best way to get a handle on this principle is to read Mark 5:21–43. We will then examine three additional passages to illustrate the principle.

Mark 5:21–43 is actually two stories, one set inside the other.[1] They form the climax for a series of miracles that began in 4:35 (Jesus calms the storm) and continued into chapter 5 (Jesus exorcises a man possessed by many demons). By the end of chapter 5, the reader has seen Jesus command nature, give orders to a multitude of demons, heal the sick with a touch of his garment, and raise the dead.

Mark shows us four scenes that clearly answer the question, "Who is Jesus?" The last two stories (a woman sick for 12 years and a 12-year-old dead girl) focus especially on faith, trusting Jesus as Savior. Mark then contrasts the faith of the woman and the faith of the dead girl's parents with the unbelief of Jesus' home town (Mark 6:1–6).

Applying the first principle of interpretation, does anything in Mark 5:21–43 require us to understand these two stories in a nonliteral sense? In other words, does Mark indicate in the text that we should take these two stories as a metaphor or in a figurative way? If not, then we can conclude that Mark thought of these stories as actual events in real history. He presents them to us as a straightforward account of what really occurred when a sick woman interrupted Jesus' journey to help a dying girl.

Some people believe that miracles can't happen. They work on the principle that "if I haven't seen it, it can't be true." They read these stories about Jesus and try to draw some "spiritual truth" from what they consider to be a myth. However, without the miraculous nature of these healings, we lose Mark's whole point. Mark wants to show the reader that Jesus is the Christ (Mark 8:29), the Son of God (Mark 15:39).[2]

In order to show us that we can trust Jesus as the woman and the girl's parents trusted Jesus, these events really had to happen (which is how Mark presents them). Otherwise we would have to say that Mark was asking us to trust in someone who couldn't help us. Neither Jesus nor Mark is promising that we won't get sick and die. That happens to Christians all the time.

Mark's point is this: Jesus has power over nature and demons, over sickness and death. God then invites us to trust in Jesus, who rescues us from our biggest problem: sin, and the righteous wrath of God against sinners. Thus Mark records Jesus' comforting words to the woman in 5:34: "Daughter, your faith has healed you. Go in peace and be freed from your suffering."

You can use the Old Testament to confirm this interpretation. It contains a number of laws dealing with ceremonial cleanness and uncleanness (see especially Leviticus 11–15). The rule is this: If you touch something unclean (or it touches you), you are rendered unclean and must go through the purification process (Leviticus 5:2). Yet a woman with a flow of blood (which renders her ceremonially unclean) touches Jesus, and Jesus touches a dead girl (also ceremonially unclean) without Himself becoming unclean. In fact, the opposite happens—the unclean people are cured of what made them unclean. Who is Jesus that he can do this? Mark answers this question in Peter's confession ("You are the Christ"—8:29) and the centurion's statement ("Surely this man was the Son of God"—15:39).

Some people have a world view that excludes the possibility of the supernatural. Others believe no divine intervention is possible in the daily affairs of the world. When these people read the miracle stories in the Bible, they cannot accept them at face value. These Bible readers are bound to misunderstand Scripture. The authors of Scripture (Mark included) present the miracles as fact. Since nothing in the context compels us to understand the words in some other way, we, too, take these words of Scripture in the normal, intended sense—as fact.

## Matthew 28:1–10

We look next at Matthew 28:1–10, where Matthew records the resurrection of Jesus. Based on the story in this section, answer the following:

1. What day of the week is it?
2. Who goes to the tomb of Jesus?
3. Who comes to the tomb ahead of them?
4. What unusual events accompany his arrival?

5.    What message does he bring?

6.    Whom do these women meet on the way back to the disciples?

7.    Why is the women's fear turned into joy?

8.    Where is the body of Jesus?

9.    How does your answer to the previous question affect your expectation, if any, for your own physical resurrection on Judgment Day?

An angel came to Jesus' tomb, rolled the stone back, and announced that Jesus had risen from the dead. The women ran away from the tomb, but on the way to the disciples they met Jesus, who spoke to them. The story is straightforward, narrated as factual history. The text contains no indication that anything is to be taken figuratively or symbolically. The problem for the modern reader does not lie in what the text says, but in whether he or she believes that the Bible is absolutely true. If you believe that it is true, you accept as truth that angels exist and you believe in the possibility of a physical resurrection from the dead. This belief has a profound impact on how you interpret and understand the story.

## Matthew 26:17–35

Human reason can be a valuable tool in Bible study. We use our human reason and study skills to explore the text. However, the use of reason has its limits. It must remain subject to God's Word. Thus, we do not place ourselves above the text. Rather, we place ourselves under the Scripture, relying on the power of the Holy Spirit to create, sustain, and build our faith, and we use reason only to help understand the intended meaning. Note how the use of reason affects the interpretation of Matthew 26:17–35. Answer the following questions:

1.    During which Jewish festival does Jesus eat the Last Supper?

2.    What does Jesus say when He gives His disciples the bread?

3.    What does Jesus say when He gives His disciples the wine?[3]

In this account of the Last Supper, Jesus says, "Take and eat; this is My body" (verse 26). He also says, "This is My blood of the covenant, which is poured out for many for the forgiveness of sins" (verse 28). The words are plain enough, but what do they mean? Is there any reason to believe that they mean something different? If we come to the text with open minds, we see that Jesus means what He says, "This is My body … this is My blood of the covenant." Answer the following:

1.    What significance does Passover have for the Jews? You may want to read Exodus 11–13 for more background. Why is it helpful to know this?
2.    What does Jesus mean when He says, "This is My body"?
3.    What does Jesus mean when He says, "This is My blood"?
4.    Can we humanly comprehend the text? Should we explain what we don't understand in human terms?

Sometimes we use the word *is* to mean *represents.* We might hold up a picture of a child and say: "This is my daughter." What we mean, of course, is "This is a picture of my daughter." In a way, the picture represents the person who is in it. We are able to figure out the meaning of the word "is" by context. If someone holds up a picture, we have no problem understanding what is meant because the photograph or painting is right in front of us. But what if we are on the other side of a door when we hear someone say, "This is my daughter"? We can't see if that person is pointing to an individual or to a photograph. Quite naturally we would assume the person is referring to his actual daughter.

When we read in Matthew's gospel that Jesus said, "This is My body," we have to determine what He meant by *this.* From the immediate context it is clear *this* refers to the bread. Further, since the text does not provide any clues that Jesus means something else than the plain meaning of the words, we should take the Words of Institution to mean that Jesus offers His body in, with, and under the bread He gives to His disciples.

We do not know how this happens or even how this is possible.

These simply are the words Matthew wrote. He provides no textual clues to indicate that we should take it any other way. Our human reason might argue that this is not possible because we can't do it ourselves. Therefore, we let Scripture be the authority and the human mind be its servant.

How can readers check their understanding of a text—apply, as it were, a kind of quality control? After reading a passage and drawing a conclusion about its meaning, we might ask, "What if the writer had said it differently?" This question assumes that the Holy Spirit inspired the various authors of Scripture to write in the clearest manner possible, expressing the intended meaning as plainly as they could. Each word, each sentence, then, becomes integral to the meaning of a verse or text.

## Matthew 28:16–20

Take, for example, the Great Commission in Matthew 28:16–20. Answer the following questions:

1. Where and when did Jesus give the Great Commission?
2. With what authority does Jesus give this commission?
3. To whom does Jesus give this commission?
4. How are Jesus' followers to make disciples?
5. What does Jesus promise at the end?

Here Jesus commissions His *listeners* to "make disciples of" all nations by baptizing them in the name of the Triune God and by teaching them to obey everything He has commanded His disciples. Jesus meant what He said—all nations—which includes people of all races, ages, and personalties.

Jesus makes no distinctions based on age, sex, ethnic background, or other such things. Sent by the Father, Jesus sends His disciples out into the world to make more disciples. He directs them to do this by baptizing and by teaching. If we have previously made up our minds that infants should not be baptized, we will not understand the Great Commission as Jesus intended it. Often the difficulty in interpreting a text lies not in the words, but in the attitudes and presuppositions of the reader.

All of us have opinions and beliefs about God, Jesus, and what is going on in the Bible. Sometimes those get in the way of understanding a text as its author intended. As hard as it is to do, we have a better chance of getting the point of a passage if we keep our minds as open as possible and pay attention to what the author actually writes in the section we are studying.

Finally, the Bible should make sense. It was written for the purpose of being read and in leading the reader to Jesus Christ as Savior and Lord, as John says in John 20:30–31. God inspired men to write the book in the language of the people so ordinary, common people would see and believe in Jesus. Except for a few sections where God apparently chose to communicate in a unique way for a specific reason (like parts of Zechariah, Ezekiel, Daniel, and Revelation), the Bible is not written in some code that requires experts to explain it to the rest of us.

The message of the Bible is, in many ways, a simple message of sin and grace, Law and Gospel, written so that the average person can understand. Jesus Himself says: "I praise You, Father, Lord of heaven and earth, because You have hidden these things from the wise and learned, and revealed them to little children" (Matthew 11:25). Thus, the first principle of Biblical interpretation is *stick to the plain and obvious meaning of the text.*

## Notes to Chapter 1

1  This technique is called intercalation, or sandwiching. The story-teller interrupts the first story to tell a second, thereby increasing dramatic tension as the audience waits for the end of the first story.

2  These are the two "high points" of Mark's Gospel.

3  This is fermented, alcoholic wine. The same word for "wine" in Matthew 26 occurs in Mark 2:22, where the production of carbon dioxide (a by-product in the making of alcoholic wine) bursts a brittle wineskin. That the wine which Jesus drank contained alcohol may also be demonstrated by Luke 7:33–34, where Jesus drinks wine and is slandered as a "drunkard."

# Scripture Interprets Scripture

## Defining the Principle

"Measure twice and cut once." This advice, given by older carpenters to younger apprentices, helps the Bible student as well. We want to make sure we have the right understanding of a particular passage, so we check our understanding of it against another, similar passage ("measure twice"). We might also think of principle #2 as a type of quality control, where we see if we have the right understanding.

THE SECOND PRINCIPLE IS THAT PASSAGES DEALING WITH THE SAME TOPIC CAN BE USED TO EXPLAIN AND SUPPORT EACH OTHER. THUS, CLEAR PASSAGES HELP US UNDERSTAND DIFFICULT ONES.

## Applying the Principle

### First Corinthians 15

In chapter 1 we read about the resurrection of Jesus (Matthew 28:1–10). The plain meaning of the text was that Jesus physically rose from the dead on the third day after His death and burial. To check our understanding, we turn to 1 Corinthians 15. Throughout this long chapter (58 verses), Paul writes about the resurrection of Jesus and what it means. Based on verses 1–8, answer the following questions:

1.   What is the heart of the Gospel (mentioned in verses 1 and 2)?
     See verses 3 and 4 for the answer.
2.   What does Paul mean by the phrase "according to the Scriptures"
     (verses 3–4)?
3.   How does Paul confirm the physical resurrection of Jesus to
     his readers? See verses 5–7.

When you answer the second question, it may be helpful to read some of the introduction to First Corinthians in the *Concordia Self-Study Bible* (pages 1744–46), especially "Author and Date" (page 1744). Paul probably wrote First Corinthians in A.D. 55, before the gospels of Matthew, Mark, Luke, and John were written and circulated. This helps us understand the phrase "according to the Scriptures" as a reference to Old Testament prophecy. Thus, Paul tells us that the death and resurrection of Jesus were prophesied in the Old Testament. Paul confirms the physical resurrection of Jesus by

* affirming this is what he was told (15:3–4);
* listing eyewitnesses (15:4–7);
* pointing out the consequences if Jesus had
  not been raised (15:12–19); and
* pointing out the consequences of Jesus' resurrection (15:20–24).

## First Corinthians 11–14

Using Scripture to interpret Scripture helps us understand the Lord's Supper as well. In chapter 1 we used Matthew 26:17–35 to illustrate interpretation based on the plain and obvious meaning of the text. Also, we find other Scripture to support that interpretation, in this case 1 Corinthians 11:17–34.

The church in Corinth suffers from a number of problems, including conduct at worship services. Paul addresses these problems in 11:3–14:40. In 11:17–34 he speaks directly to their celebration of the

Lord's Supper and outlines the problem in 11:17–22. Based on verses 17–34, answer the following questions:

1. How have divisions within the congregation affected their celebration of the Lord's Supper?
2. Where does Paul begin when he addresses the issue (11:23–26)?
3. Against what does a person sin when taking the Lord's Supper unworthily?
4. Why are many Corinthian Christians sick and weak, and why have some "fallen asleep"?
5. What things should a person do before taking the Lord's Supper?

Paul recognized the many divisions within the Corinthian church in chapter 1 (verses 10–17). He appealed to the members to heal their divisions and unite their minds and thoughts in Jesus Christ (1:10). These divisions are connected with most of the problems Paul writes about in this letter, including their observance of the Lord's Supper. For various reasons (which Paul does not mention), members of the Corinthian church arrive at their place of worship at different times. As strange as it seems, some of those who arrive early eat and drink the elements of the Lord's Supper, and as a result later arrivals don't get any and the early arrivals actually get drunk from drinking all the wine!

When Paul corrects the Corinthians, he makes a point of repeating the Words of Institution (11:23–25). Paul's understanding of the Lord's Supper is based on the words Jesus spoke when He handed the bread and wine to His disciples. This helps us check our interpretation of Matthew 26. Paul writes (in 1 Corinthians 11:27) that someone who eats the bread or drinks the cup of the Lord in an unworthy manner will be guilty of sinning against the body and blood of the Lord Jesus Christ, not merely of abusing bread and wine. Paul had already written about this connection between the body of Jesus and the bread, as well as the wine of the Lord's Supper and the blood of Jesus, in 10:14–22. He now specifically directs Christians to examine themselves before taking the Lord's Supper because the body and the blood of Jesus are really present with the bread and wine. Some Christians at Corinth have already suffered for their misuse of the Lord's Supper. Some have gotten sick, some have become weak, and some have "fallen asleep," that is, died. Paul adds that if these Christians had "judged" the Lord's Supper correctly, God would not have had to "judge" them by such severe discipline as sickness and death. Nevertheless, God did discipline them so that they would not be damned on the Last Day (1 Corinthians 11:32). Like a loving Father, God loves with a "tough love" because the stakes are so high.

## "Son of Man"

The second principle of interpretation, that Scripture interprets Scripture, has helped us check our understanding of the resurrection account in Matthew as well as his record of the Last Supper. We see another way Scripture interprets Scripture in Jesus' use of the phrase *Son of Man*. In Mark's gospel Jesus uses it first in Mark 2:10 and for the second time in 2:28. In the Old Testament this phrase usually means *human being,* as in Psalm 8:4. There the psalmist sets *son of man* in the second line of the verse, parallel to *man* in the first line. The two terms are roughly equivalent in this psalm. Similarly, in Ezekiel God uses *son of man* to address the prophet (as in Ezekiel 2:1). The term emphasizes the humanity of the prophet, particularly in contrast to the divinity of God. But is that all Jesus means when He calls Himself the *Son of Man?*

The first time Jesus uses this phrase in Mark, He says, "But that you may know that the Son of Man has authority on earth to forgive sins …" (Mark 2:10). The second time Jesus calls Himself by the title, He says, "So the Son of Man is Lord even of the Sabbath" (2:28). We can readily see that Jesus has more in mind than *Son of Man* = *human being* in these two verses! The power to forgive sins and the authority to judge what is and is not acceptable on the Sabbath ordinarily do not rest with man but with God. As we read through Mark's gospel, we eventually come to the key passage that helps us unlock what Jesus means by *Son of Man*. In Mark 14:62, when the high priest asks Jesus directly if He is the Christ, the Son of the Blessed

One (that is, the Son of God), Jesus answers, "I am." And He adds, "And you will see the Son of Man sitting at the right hand of the Mighty One and coming on the clouds of heaven."

Jesus quotes Daniel 7:13–14, where the prophet sees a vision of the Last Day. On that day of universal judgment the ultimate judge is described as "one like a son of man" who comes with the authority of God to judge all people of all nations and rule over an everlasting kingdom. By quoting this passage, Jesus reveals what He has in His mind when He says *Son of Man*. Jesus declares Himself to be that divine judge of all people on the Last Day, the "ultimate referee" who has the authority to forgive sins or not to forgive. He has divine authority to decide what is right and wrong behavior on the Sabbath day. By allowing Scripture to interpret Scripture, we find that "Son of Man" means much more than merely human; it means that Jesus is the divine judge of all the living and the dead.

# Pay Attention to the Context

## Defining the Principle

What do you do when you put a jigsaw puzzle together? Probably you look at the picture on the box. You have a better chance of getting the right piece in the right place if you can see the "big picture." So it is with Scripture. We explain the parts in light of the whole.

We recognize that the largest context is the whole of the Bible. The next smaller unit is the context of a single author or a single book. (Some authors, like James, wrote only one epistle; others, like Paul, wrote thirteen.¹) The next smaller context is the paragraph, although some literary units in Scripture are somewhat larger than this. When pastors are trained to examine the context, they often are warned that "a text without a context is a pretext." People can make the Bible say almost anything they want it to say if they quote a passage out of context. Even Peter recognizes this. Writing about Paul's letters, Peter says, "His letters contain some things that are hard to understand, which ignorant and unstable people distort, as they do the other Scriptures, to their own destruction" (2 Peter 3:16b).

THE THIRD PRINCIPLE IS TO EXPLAIN THE PARTS IN LIGHT OF THE WHOLE.

# Applying the Principle

### Romans 3:28

For our first example of precisely this point, let's take a look at Romans 3:28. There Paul writes: "For we maintain that a man is justified by faith apart from observing the law." Based on Romans 3:21–31, answer the following questions:

1. What is the righteousness of God?
2. How much of the human race has sinned and fallen short of the glory of God?
3. How much of the human race has been justified by Jesus' death and resurrection?
4. What problem did the cross of Christ solve?
5. Since God is one, how many plans of salvation can He have?

Paul uses a number of words that we don't often use. As a result, we may not clearly understand what he means when he uses them. For example, the word *righteousness* is an abstract noun that denotes the quality of being right or of doing the right thing. When used as an adjective in Scripture, it refers to the man or woman who keeps the entire Law of God. Ezekiel describes what it means to be righteous (18:5–9).

When used to describe God, *righteous* means that God always keeps His Word. God does what He says He is going to do. Yet when we read the Old Testament, we might think that God sometimes breaks His Word. We read in Genesis 2 that God permitted Adam to eat from all the trees in the garden of Eden except for the tree of the knowledge of good and evil, "for in the day that you eat of it you shall surely die" (2:17 *NKJV*).

In Genesis 3:1–6 the serpent contradicts God's Word, claiming that Adam and Eve will not die if they eat from the tree. Eve chooses to doubt God's Word, eats from the tree—and does not die. Adam was with her, watching, and when she does not die he, too, eats from the fruit of the tree. He does not die either. Even after God confronts them in Genesis 3, they do not die. In fact, Adam lived 930 years before death claimed him (Genesis 5:5).

In light of these events, can God be charged with "unrighteousness"? That is, can He be charged with failing to keep His Word? And what of all the other sins that seemingly went unpunished from the time of Adam to Christ? Paul refers specifically to this point when he writes that God punishes all sins in the person of Jesus Christ on the cross, demonstrating His righteousness (sometimes translated *justice,* as in Romans 3:25). In the cross of Christ we see God's righteousness, for in the cross of Christ He punishes all sins, even those of Adam and Eve.

It is in the cross of Christ that we also see God's grace, freely justifying sinners through faith in Jesus. Note that *justify* means *to declare righteous.* This is more than merely declaring someone *innocent* or *not guilty.* In Christ crucified God declares us righteous. He gives us credit for fulfilling the Law in every respect and for never violating it (see Ezekiel 18:5–9). God places our sin upon Christ and, through faith in Jesus, credits us with having kept the entire Law. Therefore Paul writes in Romans 3:28, "For we maintain that a man is justified by faith apart from observing the law."

## James 2:24

If this is right, then how can James say: "You see that a person is justified by what he does and not by faith alone" (James 2:24)? The answer lies in the different contexts of Romans 3 and James 2 and in the way each writer uses the verb *justify*. James is showing the connection between a living faith in Jesus Christ and the works that a Christian with such faith does. James emphasizes the external evidence of the internal faith so much so that he can define true religion as taking care of widows and orphans in their distress and in avoiding the immorality of the world (James 1:27). The good deeds done by believers show their faith to the world. Where there are no good deeds, there is no faith. Where there is faith, there are good deeds (acts of compassion and kindness, especially to fellow Christians—see James 2:14–17).

What role do these good deeds play in someone's salvation? They are the evidence of faith. As such they serve as a legal exhibit on the Last Day. On that day of final judgment, when Jesus judges the living and the dead, He will point to these compassionate applications of saving faith as evidence for a person's eternal destiny.

Jesus presents this same picture in the story of the sheep and the goats (Matthew 25:31–46). God separates the sheep and goats before He describes their deeds. Their eternal destiny is already known. The sheep receive their inheritance—eternal life—through their faith in Jesus, which they demonstrated through acts of caring. The goats, on the other hand, receive their eternal punishment because they do not have faith in Jesus. God does not proclaim great evil in their lives, but their lives reflect no saving faith in any acts of compassion done to Jesus' followers. If the word *justify* can refer to this public proclamation of judgment, then we can understand how James can say that "a person is justified by what he does and not by faith alone" (James 2:24).

When Paul uses the verb *justify,* he refers to God's declaration that all people are righteous (Romans 3:23–24) through the sacrifice of Christ Jesus. Paul also uses the word *justify* to refer to that moment when an individual is declared right with God through faith in Jesus (Romans 3:26,

28). Paul refers to what we term *justification* and James refers to that public proclamation of judgment that is based on what we call *sanctification*. If we misunderstand Paul in Romans 3:28, we might think that we can live our lives in an immoral or selfish way and it would make no difference. If we misunderstand James in James 2:24, we might think that we are partially or entirely responsible for our own salvation because of our good works. Reading Paul and James in the light of their contexts (Romans 3:21–31; James 2:14–26), we realize that they are emphasizing two different parts of the Christian's life with God, both of which are important.

## Matthew 19

Look next at the importance of context in Matthew 19. Read Matthew 19:16–28 and answer the following questions:

1. How does someone enter eternal life according to Jesus in verse 17?
2. What does it take to be a perfect disciple of Jesus according to Jesus in verse 21?
3. Under the theory that God loves rich people the most (because He has given them the most material blessings), a rich man is the "most likely to succeed" when it comes to entering the kingdom of God. What does Jesus say about the chances that even the best of us can earn our way into the kingdom according to verse 24?
4. How do the disciples respond to Jesus' statement in verse 24? (See verse 25.)
5. What does Jesus then say in verse 26 about any person's chances of earning eternal life?

If we take the question of the rich young man and Jesus' answer out of context, we might think that we have to keep all the commandments of God and sell everything and give our money to the poor in order to enter the kingdom of God and inherit eternal life. After all, that's exactly what Jesus says in verses 17 and 21. However, this teaching directly contradicts the rest of Scripture where we learn that we are saved by faith in Jesus Christ alone (as is clearly taught in Romans 3:28 and Ephesians 2:8–9). So how should we understand the responses of Jesus in Matthew 19:17 and 21?

The rich young man believes that he can do good works and thus earn God's approval. He has not been able to achieve peace with God by this method, however. He thinks he has fulfilled all the commandments, but still searches for assurance of salvation. He comes to Jesus in hopes of finding that assurance and that peace.

The Pharisees in Matthew 19:1–12 also have come to Jesus with a question, but they are not seeking peace. They hope to trap Jesus in a difficult question, in the same geographical area where John the Baptist was arrested for criticizing the marriage of Herod Antipas to his sister-in-law, Herodias. John lost his head, and perhaps the Pharisees want Jesus to get into the same trouble.

Both the rich young man and the Pharisees share a common assumption: you can earn God's approval. The Pharisees believe that Deuteronomy 24:1–4 permitted divorce under some circumstances and debated what those circumstances were. Jesus reminds them that God's original plan had been that a man and woman marry and stay married all their lives together. Jesus does something quite similar with the rich young man. By answering as He does, He confronts the rich young man with the impossibility of fulfilling the Law, just as the Pharisees were confronted with their own opposition to God's plan in 19:1–12.

The Pharisees go away frustrated and the rich young man goes away disappointed, because Jesus used the Law as a mirror to show them that their whole way of thinking was wrong. Nobody enters the kingdom of God because he or she has earned God's stamp of approval. Jesus agrees with the disciples that it is absolutely impossible for us to save ourselves from God's wrath on judgment day (19:26). But Jesus does not stop with the words, "With man this is impossible." He adds, "But with God, all things are possible." This, then, is the key to the chapter. Sandwiched between the story of the Pharisees with their question about divorce and the story of the rich young man with his question about earning eternal life we find a short story that may at first seem out of place. In Matthew 19:13–15 Jesus receives little children and says that "the kingdom of heaven belongs to such as these." With that, He places his hands on them and blesses them.

God's approval comes not through keeping the commandments or even in selling all we have and giving our money to the poor. God's approval, and thus eternal life, comes through Jesus Christ. He receives those who trust in Him, blesses them, and brings them into the kingdom of God. Jesus' disciples were shocked by His answer to the Pharisees (19:10) and panicked by His conversation with the rich young man (19:27). They even tried to prevent the little children from reaching Jesus (19:13). In short, they did not understand that human beings have no hope of earning eternal life by their good works.

Matthew writes these three stories so that we, the readers of his gospel, might understand what the disciples failed to understand. The context of the chapter makes it clear why Jesus tells the rich young man what He does in 19:17: Jesus shows him the Law with its impossible demands in order to drive him to the Gospel of full and free acceptance by grace through faith in Jesus Christ.

## Mark 4:10–12 and Isaiah 6:9

In the first part of this chapter (James 2:24 and Romans 3:28) we saw how some writers use the same words with slightly different meanings and how the whole of Scripture provides a "safety net" for interpreting those passages. In the second part (Matthew 19:17) we saw how the entire chapter helps us understand a particular verse. In the third and final part of this chapter we will see that checking out the Old Testament context of a New Testament citation helps us understand the meaning of the verse. We will look at Mark 4:12, where Jesus speaks His reason for using parables, and consider the context of the Old Testament citation—Isaiah 6:9.

Read Mark 4:10–12 and answer the following questions:

1.     Who or what does Jesus call "the secret of the kingdom of God"?
2.     Why does Jesus teach in parables?
3.     What Old Testament passage does Jesus quote?

The first extended parable of Jesus appears in Mark 4 (parallel passages are Matthew 13:1–15 and Luke 8:4–10). It seems that Jesus did not use parables (or at least none are recorded) in the early months of His ministry. Only after opposition developed (see Mark 3:6 where the Pharisees and Herodians plot together to kill Him) did Jesus begin to use parables. This provides the background for Jesus' statement in verses 11 and 12.

Two groups of people spend time near Jesus—His disciples and His enemies. To the disciples Jesus explains what the parables mean. To them He reveals the "secrets" of the kingdom of God—that He is the Messiah who has come to give His life on the cross as a ransom for all people. Jesus' enemies are waiting for Him to say something so that they may charge Him in court with a crime, preferably a capital crime. When Jesus teaches the Good News, that He is the promised Messiah, He does so covertly so that these enemies have no ammunition to use against Him in a religious or criminal court of law. Because His enemies have hardened themselves against Him, Jesus uses parables.

The Old Testament passage He cites in support of this approach is Isaiah 6:9. This verse comes from the section where Isaiah receives his call to be a prophet from God. God warns him that the people of Israel will not listen to his message or respond to his call for repentance, for they have hardened themselves against God and His Word. The preaching of God's Word, both Law and Gospel, will have the same effect on these people of Isaiah's day—it will make their minds even more closed to God's message. They have chosen this path; it is nobody's fault but their own. The key question for Isaiah to ask is simply, "For how long, O Lord?" (Isaiah 6:11).

God answers that this hardening is temporary, and that after the Assyrians have devastated Israel and the Babylonians have led Judah away into captivity, He will continue to keep His promise to send a Savior, the Messiah (Isaiah 6:13). Here we also have the key to interpreting Mark 4:12.

Jesus will advance to the cross. Using the opposition of His enemies, He will see to it that He is crucified according to the timetable He established before the foundation of the world. It would not do for Him to be rushed to the cross prematurely, before He finished the work the Father sent Him to do in His earthly ministry. By teaching in "code"—that is, by using parables—Jesus retains control of the situation and control of His destiny. When that destiny is accomplished—when He has given His life as the sacrifice for the sins of the world—then the "secrets" of the kingdom of God will be proclaimed openly for all people to see and perceive, hear, and understand. In short, the hardening of His larger audience is temporary.

The context of Mark 4 confirms this interpretation. In verse 22 Jesus predicts, "For whatever is hidden is meant to be disclosed, and whatever is concealed is meant to be brought out into the open." In both Mark 4:9 (which sets up the quote from Isaiah) and in Mark 4:23 (which marks the end of a literary unit that began at 4:9), Jesus says, "He who has ears to hear, let him hear." Scripture clearly teaches that God "wants all men to be saved and to come to a knowledge of the truth" (1 Timothy 2:4). When Christ dies on the cross, He dies for all people (Romans 3:23–24). The fact that Jesus recognizes the hostility of His enemies and avoids their traps does not contradict His love for people, including those who oppose Him. Mark reminds us (in 4:12) that Jesus is master of the situation and that He can even use people who want to see Him dead to work out His plan of salvation.

# A Key to Interpretation

We close this chapter with one more point: whenever we read Scripture and interpret it in a way that robs us of our assurance of God's love in Christ Jesus, or when we misunderstand a passage so that we lose the conviction that we are truly saved by grace through faith in Jesus Christ, we have gotten off on the wrong track. God gave us the Bible to lead us to faith in Jesus Christ and thus to have life in His name (John 20:30–31). Paying attention to the context as we interpret Scripture will help us to realize the joy of our salvation, which is so very precious to each of us.

## Note to Chapter 3

1 Some suggest that Paul wrote 14, counting the epistle to the Hebrews as his.

# Interpret Scripture in Light of the Rule of Faith

## Defining the Principle

This principle emphasizes the unity of Scripture. The whole of Scripture—all 66 books of the Bible—defines the rule of faith, that is, what God's people believe about God and His salvation.

Even though many different people wrote the Bible over a period of fifteen hundred years or so, the Bible is ultimately one Word of God. We properly distinguish Law and Gospel in this Word and we appreciate the diversity of material within this Word, but we also confess that the Bible possesses a fundamental "one-ness." In this chapter we will examine two places where New Testament authors cite the Old Testament, and then examine two New Testament passages where Jesus seems to say opposite and contradictory things.

THE FOURTH PRINCIPLE IS TO INTERPRET SCRIPTURE IN LIGHT OF THE RULE OF FAITH.

New Testament writers use the Old Testament in a variety of ways. Sometimes a New Testament writer merely *alludes* to an Old Testament text, referring to a person or an event without actually quoting the text. For example, Jesus refers to the time when David, on the run from King Saul, ate the consecrated bread at the tabernacle (1 Samuel 21:1–6). Jesus does not quote the Old Testament, but refers to the fact that David ate the forbidden bread out of necessity, confirming His point about what was legal or illegal on the Sabbath (Mark 2:23–28).

At other times Jesus *quotes* the Old Testament. For example, when Satan tempted Jesus, Jesus cites Deuteronomy three times, treating Scripture as authoritative and as a powerful tool against the devil (Matthew 4:1–11 and Luke 4:1–13). Even Satan quotes Scripture in an effort to drive a wedge between the Father and the Son.

In one case a New Testament author quotes another New Testament passage as authoritative Scripture. In 1 Timothy 5:18 Paul writes, "For the Scripture says, 'Do not muzzle the ox while it is treading out the grain,' and 'The worker deserves his wages.'" The first quote is from Deuteronomy 25:4, but the second citation never appears in the Old Testament. It matches exactly, however, a statement of Jesus in Luke 10:7.

# Applying the Principle

## Isaiah 7:14

Sometimes the meaning of an Old Testament passage doesn't become clear until the New Testament uses it. See, for example, Isaiah 7:14, which Matthew quotes in 1:23. Following good practice, we look first at the original context of the Old Testament citation. Ahaz was king of Judah when the events of Isaiah 7 unfolded. Two kings to the north (Syria and Israel) formed an alliance against the nation of Assyria and wanted Judah to join them. When Ahaz refused, the two northern nations planned to invade Judah and establish their own puppet king. Isaiah reminded Ahaz of God's promise and warned against Ahaz inviting Assyria to help him out against the two northern kingdoms. Asked to pick a sign as confirmation of God's dependability, Ahaz refused. As a result the Lord Himself chooses the sign: "The virgin will be with child and will give birth to a son, and will call him Immanuel" (Isaiah 7:14).

Over the years quite a lot of ink has been spilled over what this passage means. What did Isaiah mean by *virgin?* Who was this virgin? When did she or would she live? Not until the New Testament does the meaning become clear. When Matthew recounts the birth of Jesus, he quotes Isaiah 7:14. He tells us that Mary became pregnant before she had any sexual contact with a man (confirmed in Luke 1:34). Mary conceived Jesus by the power of the Holy Spirit (Matthew 1: 18, 20; Luke 1:35) while still a virgin. Matthew then adds: "All this took place to fulfill what the Lord had said through the prophet: 'The virgin will be with child and will give birth to a son, and they will call Him Immanuel'—which means, 'God with us'" (Matthew 1:22–23).

We can summarize the sign the Holy Spirit gave to Ahaz through Isaiah almost eight hundred years earlier as follows: if you want a sign that points to God's salvation, look for the pregnant virgin. The virgin birth of Jesus fulfills the prophecy that God gave to Isaiah and that Isaiah then offered to Ahaz as proof of God's trustworthiness. God will rescue His people and preserve the Davidic line, from whom Ahaz is descended. Sadly, Ahaz rejected God's Word through Isaiah and sought an alliance with Assyria (2 Kings 16:5–18; 2 Chronicles 28:16–21).

What did Isaiah's prophecy mean to Ahaz? God promised that by the time the child Immanuel was old enough to reject the wrong and choose the right (Isaiah 7:15–16) or old enough to say "My father" or "My mother" (Isaiah 8:4), Judah's enemies would be destroyed. The age of a child who is able to do these things is usually two or three years old. As it turned out, within two or three years of the original prophecy of Isaiah 7:14 (734/35 B.C.), Syria and Israel were defeated by Assyria. How would God have dealt with these two northern nations had Ahaz believed the prophecy and not asked for help from Assyria? Only God Himself knows.

What did Isaiah's prophecy mean to Matthew? God promised to rescue His people from their sin (Matthew 1:21, a promise expressed in the name "Jesus"). When and where will God accomplish this rescue? When the virgin becomes with child and when she gives birth. Many people have come claiming to be God's Anointed One (*Messiah* from the Hebrew;

*Christ* from the Greek), God's chosen instrument for deliverance and salvation. How are we supposed to know who is truly that Chosen One? Find the One who is born of a virgin and you've found Him!

By interpreting Scripture in harmony with itself, we see that Isaiah's prophecy finds its fulfillment in Jesus, conceived and born of a virgin, who has come so that He might save us from a peril far worse than an alliance of kings who want to wage war against us. He has come to save us from our sins.

## Hosea 6:6

We can see how this principle works when Jesus quotes Hosea 6:6, as he does on two occasions: Matthew 9:13 and 12:7. In the original context, Hosea calls God's people to repentance. He reminds them that even an external observance of God's Law with its sacrifices and burnt offerings does not really describe the heart of the relationship between God and His people. Hosea writes: "For I desire mercy, not sacrifice, and acknowledgment of God rather than burnt offerings" (6:6). Based on this verse, answer the following questions:

1.    Does God command His people to make sacrifices and burnt offerings?
2.    What does God mean when He says, "I desire mercy, not sacrifice," if He wants sacrifices?
3.    What is a covenant and what does this have to do with Hosea 6:6 (see verse 7)?

The Old Testament is full of required sacrifices and burnt offerings (for example, Exodus 20:24; 23:18; Leviticus 1, 3, 4, 7, and 8). God obviously wanted sacrifices and burnt offerings, so why would He say otherwise? Interpreting a passage like Hosea 6:6 in harmony with the rest of Scripture leads us to understand that Hosea means "I desire mercy far more than sacrifice, the acknowledgment of God far more than burnt offerings." This is confirmed by David in Psalm 51. There (in verses 16–17), he writes:

You do not delight in sacrifice, or I would bring it;
You do not take pleasure in burnt offerings.
The sacrifices of God are a broken spirit,
a broken and contrite heart,
O God, You will not despise.

God seems far more interested in the faith-relationship behind the sacrifice than in the offering itself. When the relationship between God and His people is right, when they trust in Him and put their faith into action, David adds, "Then there will be righteous sacrifices, whole burnt offerings to delight You; then bulls will be offered on Your altar" (Psalm 51:19).

The covenant God establishes with His people is built upon His grace, received through faith. Faith in God shows itself in faithfulness to the covenant, external obedience flowing from internal faith. Adam lost faith and broke the covenant God had made with him (Hosea 6:7). Israel likewise broke faith, so it made little difference whether they offered sacrifices or not. At the heart of their relationship with God, Israel needed to remember their sin and God's grace. God demonstrated this in the Exodus, where He revealed Himself as their only Savior (Hosea 13:4).

When Jesus cites Hosea 6:6, he makes the same point. In Matthew 9:13 the Pharisees criticized Him for eating with tax collectors and sinners. Jesus responds by pointing out the need that these sinners have for a Savior. He then directs them to Hosea 6:6a. If the Pharisees understood Scripture, they would realize that they, too, are sinners in need of a Savior. Moreover, God delights in showing mercy and compassion. He will punish sin, but He finds joy in forgiving repentant sinners.

Explaining the First Commandment in Exodus 20:6, God said that He would punish people to the third and fourth generations of those who hate Him, but that He would show His love to a thousand generations of those who love Him and keep His commandments (faith in God and faithful living according to His covenant). One might put this in math terms: God prefers mercy to punishment by a ratio of 250 or 333 to 1. Obviously we can't say it quite like that, but we can understand that the big picture of Scripture is our sin and God's grace, brought together in the person of Jesus Christ, crucified and risen for us.

Jesus again quotes Hosea 6:6 in Matthew 12:7. Here the disciples of Jesus are picking heads of grain, rubbing them together, and blowing away the chaff. This took place on the Sabbath, and the Pharisees considered these actions to be harvesting and threshing. Since harvesting and threshing are work, and since work was forbidden on the Sabbath, the Pharisees accuse Jesus' disciples of breaking God's law. Jesus responds by referring to the time when David and his companions ate the consecrated bread at the tabernacle (Matthew 12:4), and mentions the fact that the priests work on the Sabbath and no one accuses them of wrong-doing (Matthew 12:5). He then adds Hosea 6:6, which speaks to the attitude of the Pharisees and their (lack of) faith-relationship with God.

From the context, it appears that Jesus considers His disciples innocent of wrongdoing in this matter. They did not set out to harvest with sickles, nor did they form a threshing crew. They simply took what they needed at the moment, as did David with the consecrated bread, and ate. Jesus, the Lord of the Sabbath, declares them innocent. What attitude would a person have to have to condemn these innocent men for feeding themselves? Based on Hosea 6:6, the Pharisees reveal an attitude of unbelief and covenant unfaithfulness.

As we interpreted Scripture in harmony with itself, we followed the following steps:
- Checked the original context of Hosea 6:6.
- Confirmed our understanding of Hosea 6:6 with Psalm 51.
- Applied our interpretation of Hosea 6:6 to the use that Jesus made of it in Matthew 9:13 and 12:7, being careful to look at the contexts of each of these passages.

## Matthew 10:34 and John 14:27

We will examine one more application of this principle before moving on to the next section. When we read Matthew 10:34 and John 14:27, we see an apparent contradiction. Based on these passages, answer the following:

1. According to Matthew 10:34, what does Jesus bring to the earth?
2. According to John 14:27, what does Jesus give?
3. What does Jesus mean by "peace" in each of these passages?

In Matthew 10 Jesus sends out the 12 disciples to preach the Good News of the kingdom to God's people. He warns them about the hostility they will encounter; this will be no walk in the park. He tells them that their task is very important, and He reminds them of how important they are to God. He then adds in verse 34, "Do not suppose that I have come to bring peace to the earth. I did not come to bring peace, but a sword."

In John 14:27, Jesus and His disciples are in the upper room where they are eating the Last Supper. Jesus speaks extensively (chapters 14–17) after the meal, consoling and encouraging His disciples, because they are very troubled and confused. Perhaps they expected Jesus to usher in a new age of glory at this Passover and that they would finally receive their "paychecks" for following Him. Instead, Jesus has talked about leaving them the next day, Good Friday. In this context Jesus says, "Peace I leave with you; My peace I give you. I do not give to you as the world gives. Do not let your hearts be troubled and do not be afraid."

Does Jesus bring peace or does He bring a sword? He brings both, of course. Jesus was very controversial then and He still divides households and people today. He convicts the world of sin; therefore it must hate Him (John 7:7). He claims to be the only way to the Father, and the world cannot accept that (John 14:6). The one question that divides all people of all times into two groups is the simple question Jesus asks Martha: "He who believes in Me will live, even though he dies; and whoever lives and believes in Me will never die. Do you believe this?" (John 11:25b–26).

The question "Who is Jesus?" divides the world, but the Gospel answer "Jesus is my Savior" brings peace to the believer. Jesus brings a sword to the world, but to troubled believers He brings peace with God. Furthermore, the peace He gives to believers is impossible for the world to give or even to comprehend, just as darkness cannot comprehend the light (John 1:4). Peace with God is far more than an absence of conflict in the world. Peace with God is Jesus' gift to us by means of His death on the cross, an act of love for the world (John 3:16). Once again we see how a sensitivity to context and reading the smaller parts in light of the whole of Scripture help us to acknowledge our sin, rejoice in our Savior, and understand the passages of the Bible that we are studying.

# Interpret Scripture Christologically

[Jesus said,] "You diligently study the Scriptures because you think that by them you possess eternal life. These are the Scriptures that testify of Me." John 5:39

## Defining the Principle

This principle comes from the conviction that Jesus Christ is the focal point of the entire Scripture. If somebody asks, "What is the single point towards which all of the Bible directs the reader?," the answer would be "Jesus Christ." In this section we will consider several passages that give us this answer and help us keep Christ in the center when we read Scripture.

THE FIFTH PRINCIPLE IS THAT THE ENTIRE SCRIPTURE SHOULD BE READ IN THE LIGHT OF GOD'S REDEEMING ACTIVITY IN JESUS CHRIST. JESUS IS THE CENTER AND PURPOSE OF SCRIPTURE.

## Applying the Principle

### Acts 8:26–40

Read Acts 8:26–40 and answer the following questions:

1.   Who are the two main characters in this story?

2.    What passage from the Old Testament was the eunuch reading?

3.    How could Philip hear him?

4.    Why does the eunuch want to be baptized?

The eighth chapter of Acts continues the story of how the Gospel (or Good News) of Jesus Christ spread from Jerusalem to Rome. Stephen, the first martyr, is stoned to death in Acts 7 for testifying to Jesus as the Christ, the Son of God. A persecution of Christians followed that incident. Because of the persecution, Christians were scattered throughout the Roman province of Judea-Samaria (fulfilling the promise of Jesus in Acts 1:8). The brief account of this persecution in Acts 8:1–3 contains a fair amount of irony: instead of crushing the Christian movement, persecution spread it to points outside of Jerusalem, just as Jesus had planned!

Luke continues his record with two more accounts. They form a tremendous contrast and also contain a strong element of irony. In the first incident (Acts 8:9–25), Simon the sorcerer tries to buy the power that he sees Peter and John using to throw demons out of possessed people. Since this power was a gift from the Holy Spirit, it could not be bought.

In the next account (Acts 8:26–40), Philip shares the Gospel with an Ethiopian eunuch, a court official of a country south of Egypt. He comes to faith, is baptized, and rejoices in his salvation. Contrast the Ethiopian eunuch with Simon the sorcerer and you will see a picture of a man who tried to buy what he could not (Simon) next to a picture of a man who received freely what he could not buy (the eunuch). The sorcerer, at the end of his story, is pleading for Peter's intercession so that nothing bad happens to him for trying to buy the Holy Spirit. The eunuch, at the end of his story, goes on his way rejoicing. Both men believed, but one of them lost sight of what his faith was all about. He saw the powerful gifts of the Spirit and wanted them for his own selfish purposes. The other man saw Jesus clearly in a passage from Isaiah and experienced the joy of his salvation.

The story of the Ethiopian eunuch helps us realize the importance of a Christ-centered understanding of the Bible. As the eunuch was reading Isaiah 53:7–8, Philip overheard him (as he was directed to do). This was possible because ancient manuscripts were written in capital letters with no spacing or punctuation between words and sentences. Imagine trying to read a book like that! One had to read out loud, sounding out the words. Because of this, Philip could hear the eunuch.

The eunuch was reading part of the fourth "Suffering Servant" song,[1] a prophecy about the coming Savior (Isaiah 52:13–53:12). Specifically, the eunuch was reading Isaiah's description of the trial and execution of the coming Messiah. In fulfillment of this passage Jesus stood before Pilate, refused to answer the charges against Him, and was executed. (You can check it out in Matthew 27:14; Mark 15:5; and John 18:8–10.)

Through Philip's sermon, the eunuch comes to faith in Jesus as his Savior and Lord and, as a result, seeks Baptism.[2] Acts 6:5 introduces Philip as one of the seven so-called deacons who were chosen to administer a "widows' welfare" fund in Jerusalem. We meet Philip again in Acts 8:4–5, where he, because of the persecution in Jerusalem, has gone to a city in Samaria and there preached Christ. Because of the miraculous signs Philip performed, people paid close attention to what he said. He spoke the Gospel, and people believed in Jesus. As a result "there was great joy in that city" (Acts 8:8).

## Scriptures Point Directly to Jesus

Note the parallels between this incident and the story of the Ethiopian eunuch. Philip pointed the Samaritans to Christ and later shows to the eunuch this same Savior. Both are "disadvantaged" with regard to their covenant standing.[3] Both come to faith in Christ and, at the end of their story, experience great joy. At the center of it all, prophesied by Isaiah, is Jesus Christ crucified for the sins of the world and raised to life on the third day for our justification.[4]

Philip and Jesus use the same principle of biblical interpretation. When Philip reads Scripture, he sees Jesus. This is exactly what Jesus says in Luke 24:25 when He is on the road to Emmaus with two of His disciples on the day He rose from the dead. They do not recognize Jesus because God kept them from doing so (Luke 24:16). When they express their disappointment that Jesus was crucified, He says, "How foolish you are, and how slow of heart to believe all that the prophets have spoken! Did not the Christ have to suffer these things and then enter his glory?" (24:25–26). Jesus reveals the Christ-centered principle when He says that the central point of what the prophets have written is the person, death, and resurrection of the Christ. Luke confirms this in Luke 24:27 when he adds: "And beginning with Moses and all the Prophets, He explained to them what was said in all the Scriptures concerning Himself." The *entire* Scripture points us to Christ Jesus, our Savior and Lord.

## Scriptures Point Indirectly to Jesus

In addition to pointing directly to Jesus, the Scriptures also point indirectly to Jesus. They show us patterns that later are repeated and fulfilled. For example, in the Exodus the angel of death passes over those houses that have the blood of the lamb on their door posts (see Exodus 12). The lamb is to be a male lamb in his prime, and no bones may be broken. When Jesus goes to Jerusalem for the last time in His earthly ministry, He discusses with Elijah and Moses the exodus[5] He is about to accomplish there (Luke 9:31). When Jesus dies, a male in His prime, the soldiers do not follow the normal procedure of breaking the victim's legs. Thereby Scripture could be fulfilled: "Not one of His bones will be broken" (John 19:36, quoting Exodus 12:46, also referenced in Numbers 9:12; David echoes this promise in Psalm 34:20 as well). Since the gospel of John records an instance where John the Baptist called Jesus the "Lamb of God," we can see Christ clearly in the Passover, a pattern of salvation that is fulfilled at the cross.

## Scriptures Foreshadow Jesus

We also see Christ as the center of Scripture when we note how various events in the Old Testament foreshadow Jesus and His mission. In John 3:14 Jesus reveals to a Pharisee named Nicodemus that He has come from heaven. He is to be "lifted up," a phrase that could be interpreted in a number of different ways. Jesus makes plain what He means: "Just as Moses lifted up the snake in the desert, so the Son of Man must be lifted up, that everyone who believes in Him may have eternal life" (John 3:14–15). Jesus does not say that the bronze serpent represents Him or is in some way a pattern He will follow, but He states that He will be lifted up like Moses lifted up the bronze serpent. Two points of contact emerge: (1) "Lifting up" does not refer to Jesus' resurrection from the dead or His ascension into heaven. When Jesus uses the phrase "lifted up," He refers to His crucifixion. (2) People will be rescued by believing God's promise (John 3:15).

We find the account of the bronze serpent in Numbers 21:4–9. The people of God are in the Sinai wilderness during the 40 years between the Exodus and the conquest of Canaan. Moses determined to go around Edom rather than face that nation in war. The people grew impatient and grumbled against both God and Moses. As a result, God sent poisonous snakes among them and many people died. When the people repented, they also asked Moses to intercede for them, which he did. God told Moses to make a bronze snake and put it up on a pole. Whoever looked at it, including those bitten by a poisonous snake, lived. The bronze serpent became the means God used to elicit a faith response from His people. The bronze serpent did not have the power to heal, but God did. The people of Moses' day were rescued from death by trusting in God's promise and acting on it. The bronze serpent hanging on a pole served as the means by which God accomplished this rescue.

Like the bronze serpent, Jesus explains to Nicodemus, He will be "lifted up." Jesus uses this same language again in John 12:32, where He says that He "will draw all men to Myself," perhaps alluding to the fact that the Israelites were drawn to the bronze serpent for their rescue. And, just as in Numbers 21, people will be saved by trusting in God's promise. In this case God's promise is Jesus, crucified for the sins of the world. The rescue that God accomplishes through the cross is not simply a rescue from physical death, but a rescue from God's righteous judgment against sinners. Jesus offers eternal life to all who look to Him in faith (as He says in John 3:15).

# The Central Focus of Scripture

John 20:30–31 also points to Jesus Christ as the central focus of Scripture. Here John tells us the reason he wrote his gospel. John mentions the fact that Jesus did many miracles that he did not record. John then adds, "But these are written that you may believe that Jesus is the Christ, the Son of God, and that by believing you may have life in His name."

John's purpose in writing his Gospel is identical to the purpose of the Bible as a whole. The Bible is not primarily an instruction manual for good works, although it serves admirably to that end. It is not merely the human record of religious thought among certain peoples and cultures in the Near East, although real people from that area were inspired to write it. The most important thing the Holy Spirit does through Scripture is to bring people to a personal faith in Jesus Christ as Savior and Lord. Paul links faith and works together in discussing the purpose of the Bible, but keeps faith in Jesus as the first (and primary) purpose. Writing to Timothy, Paul says, "From infancy you have known the holy Scriptures, which are able to make you wise for salvation through faith in Christ Jesus. All Scripture is God-breathed and is useful for teaching, rebuking, correcting and training in righteousness, so that the man of God may be thoroughly equipped for every good work" (2 Timothy 3:15b–17).

Each time we open our Bibles, we should ask how they point us to Jesus as our Savior and Lord. Failure to do so weakens or even removes the comfort and hope God provides in this sacred book.

## Notes to Chapter 5

1   In four places Isaiah prophesies a coming servant of the Lord who will suffer (that is, die) for the sins of the world—Isaiah 42, 49, 50, and 52–53. These poetical sections are called the "Suffering Servant" songs. Parts of the fourth song (Isaiah 52:13–53:12) appear throughout the New Testament: Matthew 8:17; Luke 22:37; John 12:38; Romans 10:16; 15:21; 1 Peter 2:22, 24; Revelation 14:5.

2   You may notice that some later Greek manuscripts add a few lines to Acts 8:36, making it clear to the reader that the eunuch believes in Jesus and seeks Baptism for that reason. How we got our Bible will be covered in chapter 16.

3 In both his gospel and the book of Acts, Luke shows a concern for outcasts and those on the bottom of the social ladder. Jews generally hated the Samaritans, and a eunuch (who could not have children) could not even fulfill the first command God gave ("Be fruitful and multiply"—Genesis 1:28). Yet these are the people brought to Christ by the Holy Spirit in Acts 8!

4 *Justification* is a legal term that not only means *to be declared innocent,* but also, in light of Ezekiel 18:5–9, declared by God to have fulfilled all our covenant obligations (such as the Ten Commandments). This "right status" is freely credited by faith in Jesus Christ, not because we are innocent or have done what the law requires.

5 English versions differ in their translation of the Greek word *exodos.* The New King James offers *decease* (that is, departure from life), and the New International Version renders it *departure.* No doubt it does refer to Jesus' coming crucifixion, but the choice of the word *exodos* certainly also calls to mind Exodus 12, when the Israelites crossed the Red Sea.

# Distinguish Law and Gospel

## Defining the Principle

THE PROPER
DISTINCTION
BETWEEN LAW
AND GOSPEL
IS NECESSARY
TO UNDERSTAND
SCRIPTURE.

Perhaps you have learned a simple formula for distinguishing Law and Gospel: in the Law God tells us what to do; in the Gospel God tells us what He has done for us. (**SOS:** The Law **S**hows us **O**ur **S**ins. The Gospel **S**hows us **O**ur **S**avior.)

That formula sounds too simple. Sometimes it is, and sometimes it isn't. In this chapter we shall examine four portions of Scripture: Genesis 2–3; Exodus 20:1–17; Ephesians 2:8–10; and Romans 6:1–14.

## Applying the Principle

### Genesis 2–3

God created Adam and Eve without sin. In this sinless state they did not need God's written law to show them the difference between right and wrong. However, in Genesis 2:17 God reveals His first "must not." He says, "You must not eat from the tree of the knowledge of good and evil." With these words God provided a way for Adam and Eve to show their love to Him—by not eating from the tree of the knowledge of good and evil.

Only a few verses later, in Genesis 3:6, we read that both Adam and Eve ate of the fruit. In so doing, they sinned. Immediately God's Law served its purpose, showing them their transgression; they stepped over the line. They responded by trying to hide from God (3:8).

During the conversation that follows, God speaks words of Gospel: "I will put enmity between you [Satan] and the woman, and between your offspring and hers; He [Jesus] will crush your head, and you will strike His heel" (3:15). Adam and Eve receive the Good News that Jesus will win the ultimate victory over Satan. This Gospel promise assures us that we can trust our Savior to grant us the salvation He earned for us on the cross.

Law and Gospel, which become prominent already in the first three chapters of the Bible, continue to serve as filters through which we read all of Scripture.

## Exodus 20:1–17

We look next at the Ten Commandments. We'll then move on to a few passages from Paul's letters where faith (Gospel) and works (Law) are distinguished and their proper relationship revealed. Finally, we'll read a passage from Luke's gospel concerning prayer and ask whether God answers prayer on the basis of Law or Gospel. We find the Ten Commandments in Exodus 20 and Deuteronomy 5.[1]

Sometimes people think they have to do good works to be saved, or that they have to keep the Ten Commandments so that God will love them. A quick check on the original context of the commandments helps us understand that God did not give us these rules so that we could save ourselves or earn His love.

God gave the commandments about one year after He rescued the Hebrews from Egypt in the original Exodus (see Exodus 19:1). Before Moses gives the people the commandments (Law), he reminds them that God has saved them by grace (Gospel): "I am the LORD your God, who brought you out of Egypt, out of the land of slavery" (Exodus 20:2; Deuteronomy 5:6).

In short, God did not give the law to the Hebrews so they could save themselves. God had done that almost a year earlier. His love for them springs from within Him, not from their obedience to the commandments. Before God gave the Ten Commandments, He had rescued them, carrying them on "eagles' wings" out of slavery and death to be with Himself (Exodus 19:4).

## The Purpose of the Law

God did not give the Law so people could save themselves, why did He give it at all? God's Law served as a guide for God's people. Now that God had rescued them from Egypt, what did He expect of them?

The New Testament often asks a similar question: now that we have been brought to faith in Jesus Christ, what are we to do with our lives? In the Old Testament as well as in the New Testament, putting our faith into practice is an important part of our calling.

In both testaments God calls His people a "kingdom of priests" and a "holy nation" (see Exodus 19:6 and 1 Peter 2:9). Priests offer sacrifices, and a holy nation is a nation of people set apart for service to God. Unlike the sacrificial victims of Old Testament days, we Christians offer our whole lives as sacrifices (Romans 12:1). We give back to God our bodies and souls and everything we have in gratitude for what Christ has done for us on the cross.

Thus, the Ten Commandments served as a guide for God's people, and God's Law continues to serve Christians in this way. The Law also shows us our sins (as stated earlier in the chapter), and curbs evil impulses with the threat of punishment.[2] But the Law cannot save.

God's Law is bigger than the Ten Commandments. Throughout the Old Testament God gives His people directives for how they are to live in society, how they are to offer sacrifices and other religious duties, and what type of morality they are to practice. Keeping God's Law entails more than avoiding sin. It involves not only avoiding the wrong, but doing the right. It includes an obligation to take care of people who need our help. We see this in both the Old Testament (Ezekiel 18:5–9) and the New Testament (James 1:27). Martin Luther highlighted this obligation in his explanations of the Ten Commandments. After the negatives ("so that we do not") he stated the positives ("but that we do").

## Ephesians 2:8–10

The proper distinction between Law and Gospel is of critical importance, because when we confuse the two we can lose the assurance of our salvation. If my salvation depends on me, even if it depends only a tiny, tiny bit on me, how can I be sure that I have done my "bit" just right?

To be absolutely sure of our salvation, we must recognize that it depends absolutely and only on Jesus Christ. The lives we lead after we are brought to faith in Jesus Christ are lived that way *because* we have been saved, not *in order to* be saved. Paul keeps the relationship between Law and Gospel in balance throughout his letters, and we can see it particularly in Ephesians 2:8–10 and Romans 6:1–11.

In Ephesians 2 Paul describes the contrast between the former life of his Christian readers and their present life. Before the Gospel came to them, they were condemned by God (as are all people by nature). Now, having come to faith in Jesus Christ, they are rescued from God's righteous anger against sinners on the Last Day. Paul describes this contrast twice, first in 2:1–10 and then in slightly different terms, 2:11–22. Read the end of the first section (2:8–10) and answer the following questions:

1. What moved God to save sinners?
2. What is the source of saving faith?
3. How do good works figure into the equation of salvation?

The Bible often mentions God's *grace*. Depending on the translation, Paul uses the term at least a dozen times in Ephesians alone.[3] We can define grace very simply as *undeserved love*. God saves sinners through faith in Jesus Christ. This is the only way of salvation in all history and in all of the world.

What moved God to send His one and only Son so that whoever believes in Him would not perish but have eternal life? God's love motivated Him, a love we do not deserve, but which He pours out on us richly in Jesus Christ (see Ephesians 2:7). By the gracious gift of God—Jesus Christ—people are saved. Note what Paul says, though; they are saved through faith. This faith is not a decision we make to believe in God, but a gift of God. Paul could hardly have said it more clearly. God gives us the faith we need to personally receive the benefits of Jesus' sacrifice on Calvary. It is important to keep this in mind, for faith is a Gospel gift, not a result of the Law.

We do make a contribution to our life with God, but that does not come at the point of conversion. God is the One who brings us into His family (Gospel); once we are members of His family, we seek to live out His will for our lives (Law). But our salvation depends entirely on what He has done and continues to do for us (Gospel).

In a sense, living the Christian life is easy. God has made us His own special people and He has even prepared good works in advance for us to do. He provides us the opportunities and the resources to help feed the hungry, speak up for the oppressed, help our neighbor, and the like. Living our lives for Jesus should be the easiest thing in the world, right? But the fact is, putting our faith into practice is very hard—even impossible when we rely upon our own power instead of the power God provides through the Gospel.

Some have compared the Christian life to dieting. We succeed (at least to a degree) for a while, but over the long haul we often seem to lose the ground we gained. We cover the same territory in our lives over and over and over. But in Christ Jesus we get up and try again, trusting Him for forgiveness and help. As we do so, we know that His love for us is secure (Gospel) and that in His strength we live out our faith according to His purpose for us on earth (Law). Even as we live, we await the time He calls us home (Gospel).

## Romans 6:1–14

Written three or four years earlier than Ephesians, Paul traces the same relationship between Law and Gospel in Romans 6:1–14. He anchors our sanctification (Christian lifestyle) in our justification (God's declaration that we are sinless and have fulfilled His covenant demands), specifically, in our Baptism. God's gift of salvation to us (Gospel) becomes our motivation for holy living (keeping the Law). Based on Romans 6:1–14, answer the following:

1.     What happens to a person in the process of being baptized?
2.     What does the resurrection of Jesus Christ from the dead
       mean to us?
3.     What kind of relationship does the Christian have with sin?

We can compare being baptized to taking a trip. We are first carried back to the death of Jesus where we are buried with Him and washed clean of our sins in His blood. We are then transported to the future, to Judgment Day, where we see God keep His promise to us in our Baptism that "he who believes and is baptized shall be saved" (Mark 16:16a). We finally return to our own time, the present day, where we live each day in a new way. We live for the glory of God and not our own welfare. We live as servants of the Lord Jesus, not as slaves to sin. We live free from the demands of the Law, filled with the Gospel, free to show Christ's love in all that we say and do.

Very soon we realize that we still struggle with sin. In Romans 7 (especially verses 14–25) Paul expresses the frustration every Christian has in trying to live the way Jesus has called us to live. But even our failure to live according to God's will (Law) does not rob us of the great comfort of knowing that our salvation is secure in Jesus Christ (Gospel). We rejoice in this, not that it should become a license for sin, but that we have a freedom from fear and are called to serve Him who gave everything for us. Keeping Law and Gospel distinct makes it possible to live in the joy of our salvation in spite of our success or failure in applying our faith to our daily lives.

# Notes to Chapter 6

1   There seem to be 11 commandments in both Exodus and Deuteronomy, but since they are called the Ten Commandments (Exodus 34:28; Deuteronomy 4:13; 10:4), we number 10. Roman Catholics, Lutherans, and some other Protestants number Exodus 20:3–5a as the First Commandment, and divide verse 17 to become the Ninth and Tenth Commandments. Many other Protestants list verses 4–5a as the Second Commandment, and keep all of verse 17 as the Tenth Commandment. God, however, does not number the commandments.

2   Lutherans traditionally number these uses of the Law as follows: the Law curbs evil impulses with the threat of punishment (first use); shows us our sins (second use); and serves as a guide for God's people (third use).

3   The same Greek or Hebrew word can often be translated with a variety of English words. When doing a word study in the Bible, it can be helpful to check several different translations.

# Part Two

## Interpreting Different Kinds of Scripture

How often do conflicts arise because friends misunderstand messages they send, including oral communication? If "here and now" communication must overcome obstacles, we certainly need the help of the Holy Spirit to understand the "then and there" communication of Scripture. What did the original speaker or author mean, and what did the original hearer or reader understand when the message was first spoken or written? Chapter 7 will address this issue.

In chapters 8, 9, 10, and 11 we will explore guidelines to follow for special kinds of Biblical writing: poetry, prophecy, parables, and apocalyptic writing. Chapter 12 provides a summary of tools available to help you study Scripture.

# The "Then and There" Meaning and the "Here and Now" Meaning

As we know from everyday life, communication can be hard work, both for the writer and the reader (or speaker and listener). It is easy to misunderstand what someone else writes or says. Bible students, too, often misinterpret passages. Let's use an absurd example to illustrate this.

*Once upon a time in a Bible study far, far away, two men were arguing about what kind of vehicle Jesus used when he rode into Jerusalem (Matthew 21). The first man argued that Jesus drove a Dodge product, because verse 7 says he rode in on a Colt and Dodge makes a car called a* Colt. *The second man argued that Jesus drove a Ford because Colt has four letters and so does the word* Ford. *He argued that* Colt *was a special code word that really meant* Ford. *Which of the two was right?*

The first man made the mistake of thinking that Jesus lived in twentieth-century America. As silly as this sounds, many people make mistakes very similar to this because they fail to realize that Jesus was a first-century Palestinian Jew who spoke to people of that region and time. The second man made the mistake of thinking that the Bible is full of secret codes, where numbers and animals and events hide secret meanings that only a few "insiders" know about. Again, this sounds very silly, but it is an approach to Bible study. We will see a symbolic use of numbers in apocalyptic writing,[1] but no such secret codes exist.

Oscar Feucht (*Learning to Use Your Bible,* CPH, 1969) offers three basic questions to ask when studying the Bible:

1.   What does the passage say?
2.   What does the passage mean?
3.   What does the passage mean to us—to me?

# What Does the Passage Say?

The first of these questions asks us to read the text carefully. Do we know what all the individual words mean? After all, words can sometimes mean many different things, depending on usage and context. Take the word *cat* as an example. When you use this word, you probably refer to a domestic house cat—small, furry, and friendly. But *cat* can also refer to the large predators of Africa and Asia such as lions, tigers, and leopards. We can also use the word *cat* figuratively, as it was in the 1960s, to refer to someone of a particular attitude and dress (a "cool cat").

Words can also have technical meanings in addition to their everyday meanings. We can use the word *prayer* to illustrate this point. Normally, prayer refers to our communication with God. But in some states, in legal contexts, *prayer* refers to the amount the plaintiff is seeking from the defendant in a lawsuit.

A particular writer may also use a word or a group of words with one specific set of meanings in mind. For example, look at the verb *to save*. This word means *to rescue* and can be used to describe various kinds of rescues. If a man is rescued from a ship or a woman is rescued from a fire, we can use the word *save* to refer to that rescue. But what about those times when Jesus says, "Your faith has saved you"? Does He mean someone has been healed because they believed in Him, or does He also mean they have been rescued from the Law's condemnation on Judgment Day because they believe in Jesus? In Luke 8:48 Jesus says, "Your faith has saved you"[2] to a woman who was healed when she touched His robe. He says the same thing to a leper who has been healed in Luke 17:19 and to a blind beggar he has healed in 18:42. It would seem that when Jesus says, "Your faith has saved you," He means, "Your faith has made you well," which is the usual translation of Luke 8:48. (See page 95.)

However, when Jesus says "Your faith has saved you" to a sinful woman in Luke 7:50, no physical healing at all had taken place. Jesus forgave her sins, which means the rescue she received from Him was a rescue from the Law's condemnation on the Last Day. She has been saved from damnation. This may well be what Jesus primarily has in mind in the other passages in Luke as well. The faith those people had in Jesus saved them from God's judgment against sinners; as a token of that, they were healed of their diseases as well.

The question "Do we know what all the words mean?" may look easy on the surface. At times, however, further study (such as applying the principles from Part One) will provide deeper insights. To avoid the mistake of the man who thought *colt* referred to an automobile made by Dodge, we need to learn that words can have a variety of meanings. To tell what an author means by a particular word, we must trace his use of it throughout his writings.

Do we know what the text says? At times Bible students overlook this basic step. Some say, for example, that Saul changed his name to Paul when he was converted. They may even claim that this change to Paul (a Latin word meaning "little") indicated his newly found humility. However, the book of Acts contains no record of such a name change. Jesus confronts Saul and converts him in Acts 9. Luke (the author of Acts) does not call him Paul until Acts 13:9, on the first missionary journey some 14 years after his conversion. Very likely Saul had the name Paul from birth, one of three Latin names a Roman citizen would normally have. In any event, no textual evidence indicates that he acquired it at his conversion. Let's not skip the first step of Oscar Feucht's Bible study advice! If we do, we can easily miss material in the text or imagine things that never really took place.[3]

# What Does the Passage Mean?

The second step is interpretation: what does this passage mean "then and there"? The answer to this question may involve some research into the historical or cultural background of the passage being studied. We can look at Matthew 1:18–19 for an example. Read these two verses and answer the following questions:

1. What is the relationship between Mary and Joseph at this time?
2. Why is Joseph called her husband?
3. What does it mean when Matthew writes, "Before they came together"?
4. What qualities of Joseph do the words *righteous man* emphasize?
5. If they are only engaged, why does Joseph have to divorce her?

Matthew begins the section by noting that Mary was engaged (betrothed, pledged to be married) to Joseph when she became pregnant. In our culture, engagement is a verbal pledge usually accompanied by the giving of a ring. A second ring is given at the wedding ceremony. The practice in first century Palestine was quite different. A written contract bound engaged couples. Thus, the betrothal period (a minimum of nine months and a maximum of one year) was very formal and was legally binding. This also explains two other details in the story. Since they were bound by this engagement contract, they could be called husband and wife, though they could not live together. If they chose to nullify the engagement contract, they could do so. We call this divorce.

This text illustrates a problem that comes up from time to time in Bible study. Matthew knows first-century Jewish laws and customs. So do his original readers. Matthew wrote in Greek, which his original audience read. We live 2,000 years removed from that time and half a world away from it. And as for Greek, very few of us know it well enough to be able to read it and understand it. This means that we must do homework when reading various parts of the Bible. This second step of Oscar Feucht's advice can challenge us.

Matthew makes it clear that Joseph did not father the baby Mary is now carrying. He writes "before they came together," an expression that refers to sexual intercourse. At the end of verse 20, we may describe the situation like this. Someone other than the man to whom she is engaged has caused Mary to become pregnant. Bound by engagement contract, the same laws that applied to married people apply to her. The Old Testament penalty for adultery[4] is death, and so Mary should be stoned according to the law (see Leviticus 20:10). However, the Romans rule Palestine at this time. They do not permit a local people to try capital cases, reserving the "right of the sword" for themselves.[5] In Roman law adultery was not a capital crime. Therefore the Jews cannot stone an adulteress. The rabbis decided that if they could not execute a woman for this crime, she must be regarded the same as dead. So they required that the husband divorce his adulterous wife.

Now, Joseph is a righteous man. This description means that he keeps the law (see Ezekiel 18:5–9). As a righteous man (one who keeps the law) he will divorce Mary, that is, void their engagement contract. Joseph's plan for the divorce reveals his character. Instead of making a public display of Mary, making sure that no one in their small village of Nazareth would blame him for the pregnancy, he plans to divorce her quietly, without a lot of fanfare. In short, he risks public embarrassment in order to minimize the shame that (he thinks) Mary will have to endure.

What have we learned about discovering the "then and there" meaning of this text? Joseph and Mary are engaged, a legally binding relationship. Mary becomes pregnant (through the miraculous activity of the Holy Spirit). Thus, in the eyes of the law she becomes an adulteress. In reality, she is a virgin, but Joseph doesn't know this yet. Joseph is a law-abiding man and will do what he is required to do, but reveals a noble character by deciding to divorce (nullify the engagement contract) Mary quietly.

As we can see, it sometimes takes work to put ourselves in the shoes (or sandals) of the original readers of the Bible. The various Bible study tools help us do this, but Bible study is really a lifelong adventure. There's always something "just around the corner" that may help us understand a passage with which we have previously struggled.

As we look for the meaning of the text, we often look for Bible teachers who can help us. As we do so, we need to remember that not everyone who stands up and says, "This is what the Greek (or Hebrew) means" is right. Human beings are often wrong.

However, someone who has spent his or her life in the Word can very often help others understand the Bible better. Note what happened to Apollos when he arrived in Ephesus. He was a learned man with a thorough knowledge of the Scriptures and taught about Jesus accurately. He was a great Bible teacher and evangelist, but he didn't know about Christian Baptism. So Priscilla and Aquila, a wife and husband team, instructed him more fully about the Christian faith (see Acts 18:24–26). No matter how much we know, there's always room to grow in the faith!

# What Does the Passage Mean to Us—to Me?

We now turn to Oscar Feucht's third question, "What does the passage mean to us—to me?" People answer this question in two ways:

- It means whatever I want it to mean.
- Stay as close to the original meaning as possible.

To illustrate these ways of answering the question, look again at Matthew 1:18–19. Some who interpret the text to mean whatever they want it to mean have concluded that God condones sexual activity before marriage but after engagement. They base this on the use of *husband* for Joseph, Mary's fiancé. If a husband may be intimate with his wife, and Joseph (who is only engaged) is called a *husband,* then God must approve intercourse between engaged couples. So the logic goes—logic based on a faulty answer to the question of what the passages means to our lives today.

To apply a passage to our lives accurately, we must stay as close to the original meaning as possible. Looking at Matthew 1:18–19, we discover that God gave us this text to relate Mary's virgin conception of Jesus by Holy Spirit. Matthew also explained why Joseph did not divorce Mary in spite of the fact that he was a righteous (law-abiding) man. As was the custom of the day, Mary and Joseph did not engage in sexual activity prior to their wedding.

In these two verses we see God at work, fulfilling His promise to send a Savior, born of a virgin (Matthew 1:23). God accomplishes salvation without any human help, even at the initial stage. We may learn from these verses that God is at work in the world and in our lives to accomplish His will, our salvation (as Paul says in 1 Timothy 2:4). God is at work in Mary's life, in Joseph's life, and in our lives to bring people to faith through the Gospel of Jesus Christ. This is true even when the events of our lives create problems (premarital pregnancy in the case of Mary) or challenge our Christian character (a pregnant fiancée for Joseph). God works all these things for the good, that is, for the salvation of His people (Romans 8:28–30).

When we read a passage in Scripture, we want to remember to ask and answer the first two questions before we apply a section of the Bible to our own lives:

1.   What does the passage say?
2.   What does the passage mean?
3.   What does the passage mean to us—to me?

## Notes to Chapter 7

1   "Apocalyptic" refers to a type of prophecy and to a literary genre where various kinds of symbolism are used.

2   Some translations use the English phrase "made you well" or "healed you" instead of "saved you."

3   Sometimes pictures in our minds prevent us from reading the text carefully. For example, the shape of the ark in Genesis 6 resembles a giant shoe box, not a ship. Yet, when the ark is mentioned, people usually think of some kind of boat. Or picture Elijah being taken to heaven. He did not travel in a fiery chariot. The text says he was taken into heaven by a whirlwind (2 Kings 2:1, 11). A fiery chariot separated Elijah and Elisha, but the whirlwind took Elijah up.

4   Adultery is a very specific crime in the Bible. It refers to a married man or woman being intimate with someone other than his or her spouse. (See Jeremiah 29:23; Hosea 3:1; and Romans 7:3.)

5   This same problem occurs in John 18:31, where the Jewish leaders must take Jesus to Pilate for execution rather than do it themselves.

# Poetry in the Bible

Poetry, like prose, comes in a variety of styles. In the ancient world, poetry was used to tell stories. Examples from Greek literature include *The Iliad* and *The Odyssey* by Homer, written in the 8th century B.C. or earlier. This kind of poetry is called *narrative poetry* because it tells a story that has a beginning, a middle, and an end. Probably written long before Homer's works, the book of Job serves as a good example of narrative poetry in the Bible.

By the fifth century B.C. poets were using poetry to write plays. Works by Euripides, Sophocles, and Aristophones fall into this category in the ancient world. Shakespeare is a more modern example of the same type of poetry. The Bible does not contain any of this kind of poems.

A third type of poetry in Bible times is lyric poetry, poems intended to be read as the lyre (a stringed musical instrument) is played.[1] The Bible has a large number of this type of poem, most notably the psalms. Some also occur in the New Testament, for example, in Luke 1 and 2. The poetry we find in the Bible has some elements in common with poetry outside of the Bible, but it also differs in many ways. The poems in the Bible aren't based on a meter that we would ordinarily recognize, and biblical poetry does not rhyme.

# Parallelism

The most obvious distinctive feature of Hebrew poetry is parallelism, a repetition of the thought in the first line expressed with some variation in the second line. The second line may be synonymous with the first line, may introduce an opposite thought, or may enrich—add emphasis—to the first line. This parallelism makes the poem (or psalm) especially useful in worship services, because it lends itself so readily to antiphonal reading or chanting. One part of the assembly says the first line and the second part of the worshiping group repeats the thought of the first line, but says it in a different way.

See Psalm 121 for any example of parallelism. The Hebrews used this psalm as a pilgrimage song, sung by people on the way to Jerusalem. In Jerusalem was the temple, the "embassy" of God on earth. As pilgrims traveled up to Jerusalem, which is set on the top of a mountain, they could sing or chant this psalm in preparation for worship and sacrifice. This wonderful Gospel poem assures the believer of God's providence and care. As you read the psalm, notice how the poet has made his song sound natural, almost like a conversation or dialogue. Each of the second lines repeat or expand the thought in each of the first lines without sounding artificial or forced.

# Historical Setting

When reading Hebrew poetry, especially the psalms, it is very helpful to know the historical setting in which the poem was written. Psalm 51 provides a very good example of this. The heading of the psalm reads: "For the director of music. A psalm of David. When the prophet Nathan came to him after David had committed adultery with Bathsheba." If you don't know the story of David, Bathsheba, Uriah, and the prophet Nathan, it is a good idea to turn to 2 Samuel 11:1–12:25. David commits a variety of sins (including adultery and murder), but tries to cover them up. Only after

more forceful. He then contrasts our apparent insignificance with the status God has granted us as His image and likeness (see Genesis 1:26–28), writing in verse 5:

> "You made him a little lower than the heavenly beings[2] and
> crowned him with glory and honor."

God created humans in His image and likeness, and appointed them as His representative to rule over the earth. The theory of evolution tells us that we are essentially the same as the animals, particularly the primates. We may be at the top of the food chain now, but only by accident have we achieved this. Genesis 1–2 (and Psalm 8) reveal to us that we were created to be the "crown of creation," God's appointed managers of the earth, second only to Him in relation to the rest of creation. Yet the gulf between us and God is very great, as the psalmist confesses. However, God often chooses the lowly things of this world to reflect His mercy and praise (Psalm 8:2).

# Messianic Psalms

Another feature of the psalms is that they are sometimes Messianic. That is, they combine prophecy and poetry to portray the coming Savior. Psalm 2[3] (part two of a two-part introduction to the whole book of Psalms) and Psalm 110[4] both serve as examples of Messianic psalms, but none is more powerful than Psalm 22. Read Psalm 22 and identify details that pertain to Christ's crucifixion, recorded in Matthew 27:45–56; Mark 14:33–41; Luke 23:44–49; and John 19:16b–30. Keep in mind this was written by David, about 1,000 years before Jesus died on the cross for the sins of the world.

Psalm 22:1 _____

Psalm 22:6 _____

Psalm 22:7 _____

Psalm 22:8 _____

Psalm 22:15 _____

Psalm 22:16 _____

Psalm 22:17 _____

Enjoy the poetry of the Bible! As the Old Testament often celebrated God's deliverance of His people in psalms (Exodus 15; Psalms 74, 77–78, 105–106), so in the New Testament several poems rejoice in the Lord Jesus Christ (two of them are Philippians 2:5–11; Colossians 1:15–20).

## Notes to Chapter 8

1 Hebrew lyric poems date back to David, about 1000 B.C. Classic Greek lyric poetry dates back to Pindar, about 500 B.C.

2 The Hebrew word here is Elohim, a word which usually refers to God. Many translators think it refers to the angels, but it makes good sense to understand it as a reference to God. By God's grace, humans were made to be His representatives on earth ("image and likeness"), second only to God in status.

3 Psalm 2:1 is quoted in Acts 4:25; 2:7 appears in Acts 13:33 and Hebrews 1:5, 5:5; and 2:9 is cited in Revelation 2:26; 19:15.

4 Jesus quotes Psalm 110:1 in Matthew 22:44; Mark 12:36; and Luke 20:42. It is also quoted in Acts 2:34; 1 Corinthians 15:25; and Hebrews 1:13. In the New Testament, it is the most often-quoted Old Testament passage. Psalm 110:4 appears in Hebrews 5:6; 7:17, 21.

# Prophecy in the Bible

## Old Testament

Old Testament prophets spoke for God. They admonished God's people, convicting them of their sins (Law). The prophets also spoke of God's mercy and compassion, encouraging the people to repent and believe (Gospel). Sometimes, during the course of their work, prophets would predict the future. One way to tell if a prophet was a true prophet or a false prophet was whether his predictions came true (Deuteronomy 18:22). This was not the only test for a prophet, however. If a prophet led the people away from the one true God, or if he prophesied in the name of another god, he was to be put to death (see Deuteronomy 13).

The office of prophet was so important as God's spokesman in the Old Testament that the coming Messiah could be described as a prophet. (See Deuteronomy 18:15–20.) Both men and women could be prophets in Old Testament times.[1]

## New Testament

The prophet in the New Testament seems to have a somewhat narrower "job description." For example, Agabus is a prophet (Acts 21:10), but seems to limit his activity to predicting future events. Most of those who prophesy reveal future events, but not all who prophesy are true prophets (as Jesus warns in Matthew 24:11 and Mark 13:22).[2] As in the Old Testament, both women and men prophesy.[3]

# Interpreting Prophecy

The modern student of the Bible needs to ask an important question when reading about prophecy: *Can a prophet, inspired by the Holy Spirit, predict the future?* In Acts 11:28 Luke records an incident where Agabus, led by the Spirit, predicted a famine. Luke also notes that this prediction was fulfilled in the reign of Claudius (who died in A.D. 54). The date of the prediction was approximately A.D. 44 (as indicated by the death of James the son of Zebedee in Acts 12). Later this same prophet, Agabus, predicts that Paul will be arrested and handed over to the Gentiles (Acts 21:10–11). His prediction is fulfilled when Paul reaches Jerusalem (Acts 21:27–36).

The testimony of God's Word is that prophecy, specifically the prediction of future events, is a gift that God gives when and where it pleases Him. Satan also "inspires" people so that they can tell something of the future (as in the case of the slave girl in Philippi, Acts 16:16–18). Yet it is only the true prophet who has the message of salvation and points people to the one true God. Thus we see that Jesus is our prophet *par excellence* (Deuteronomy 18:18; Matthew 13:57; 21:21; John 6:14).

Since the few New Testament prophetic passages are fulfilled shortly after the prophecy is given (with the exception of some passages in Matthew 24–25, Mark 13, Luke 21, and Revelation—these will be covered in chapter 11), we will consider Old Testament prophecy in this chapter. Interpretation of prophecy can be difficult. Sometimes a prophet clearly predicts a future event, quite often fulfilled centuries later in the person and work of Jesus Christ. Sometimes a prophet acts out his prophecy, like a visual aid in a children's sermon. Sometimes the New Testament sees prophetic meaning in an Old Testament event, which by itself may not seem prophetic.

# Guidelines for Interpretation

We can use three guidelines to help us understand Old Testament prophecy:

- Look for the intended meaning of the prophecy.
- See if the New Testament refers to the Old Testament passage under study.
- Understand the difference between direct (verbal) prophecy and symbolic (action) prophecy.

# Practicing the Guidelines

## Micah 5:2

The prophet Micah lived about eight hundred years before the birth of Jesus. He warned God's people to repent of their sin, turn away from idols, and give up empty ritualism. He promised God's forgiveness to those who would turn to Him in faith and looked forward to the day when God's promised Messiah would take away the sins of the world. Read Micah 5:2 and answer the following questions:

1.    Whose birth does Micah predict?
2.    Where is this person to be born?
3.    How important is the place of this person's birth?

In Micah 5:2 he predicts the birthplace of that Savior: the village Bethlehem in the region of Ephrathah in the tribal area occupied by Judah. This was an unimportant village in Micah's day, but because the Messianic king would be born there, its historical importance would be very great. This kind of prophecy is the easiest to interpret. It contains no codes or secret messages. The message is quite plain. Sometime in the future God's promised Messiah will be born in Bethlehem.

Jewish scholars had this same understanding of Micah 5:2 when the Magi came to Jerusalem looking for the one who had been born king of the Jews. The chief priests and teachers of the Bible, gathered by Herod the Great, knew exactly where the Messiah would be born (Matthew 2:1–6). These experts in the Old Testament even quoted Micah 5:2 to Herod. The prophecy seems very straightforward in Micah and (using the second guideline) our understanding is confirmed by Matthew in the New Testament.[4] This is the simplest form of prophecy—predicting a single event that Scripture later records as fulfilled.

## Jeremiah 31:15

Sometimes New Testament writers look at Old Testament events and see a pattern that resembles an incident in the life of Jesus. We will look at two examples in the second chapter of Matthew.

In Matthew 2:18 the author cites Jeremiah 31:15 and sees a connection between that verse and the slaughter of infants at Bethlehem. The wailing of the mothers for their murdered sons fulfills (or repeats) a pattern highlighted in Jeremiah 31. Rachel, favorite wife of Jacob, had been buried near the town of Ramah. Ramah was about five miles north of Jerusalem. When Babylon conquered Jerusalem, the captives were led away on a route that passed near Ramah. Jeremiah pictures Rachel, dead for more than 10 centuries, weeping for her descendants as they are taken into captivity in a foreign land (Babylon).

As we have seen before, the original context is important. Jeremiah 31:15 appears in the midst of consolation, a promise by God to bring back the captives, a message of hope and life in the midst of death and destruction. That is, of course, the same kind of situation we find in Matthew 2. In the midst of the death and destruction of the infants, the message of life and hope (Jesus Christ) shines brightly.[5]

## Hosea 11:1

Matthew also sees a pattern when Jesus and his parents returned from Egypt, where they had gone to escape Herod the Great. In 2:15

Matthew quotes Hosea 11:1, "Out of Egypt I called my son." In Hosea, the prophet refers to the original Exodus as he reminds his readers that God is calling them to repentance as a loving father calls a wayward son. The tragedy is that Israel did not listen to God's gracious invitation and continued in their idolatrous and sinful ways. Like them, Jesus travels from Egypt to Palestine. But unlike them, He follows the Law perfectly, the ideal Son. Jesus fulfills the pattern of sonship and thus fulfills an action prophecy.

## Jeremiah 31:15

Sometimes the intended meaning of a prophecy is broader than it first appears. We can use Jeremiah 31:31–34 as an example. Read this passage and answer the following:

1. To whom does God promise a new covenant?
2. How will God give them this covenant
3. What is the essence of this new covenant?

The author of Hebrews twice quotes this passage (Hebrews 8:8–12 and 10:16–17). He makes the point that this new covenant (or testament) is superior to the covenant God made with Moses for four reasons:

1. God will write this on their hearts (minds) and not on stone tablets.
2. God will establish a personal fellowship with His people.
3. God will remove all ignorance and disobedience from His people.
4. God will forgive all sins forever.

This new testament will replace the old, the author of Hebrews says. Because this prophecy looks forward to the time when the final sacrifice for sin will have been made, the new testament era contains no sacrificial system. Jesus makes the sacrifice once, for all. As is clear in both the Old and New Testaments, God intends to include Gentiles in this new covenant. This becomes evident in Paul's understanding of the Gospel (Romans 1:16–17).[6] It is also true that this promise will not be completely fulfilled until Jesus returns, judges the living and the dead, and provides the new heavens and the new earth for His people.

# The "Now" and the "Not Yet"

Living between the first and second coming of Jesus, we find ourselves in a time of joy and sorrow. We celebrate the victory of Jesus over sin, death, and the devil; yet we struggle daily with sin, fear death, and are tripped up by the devil. The end of the world has already come in the person and work of Jesus Christ; yet, somehow, we await the end of the world that is yet to come. This can create challenges for us when we interpret prophetic passages. Let us take Joel 2:28–32 as an example. Read this passage and answer the following:

1.   When does God pour out His Holy Spirit?
2.   When do all God's people prophesy, dream dreams, and see visions?
3.   When does the sun turn to darkness and the moon to blood?
4.   When is it that everyone who calls on the name of the Lord will be saved?

We might think that the answer to all these questions is "On the last day." Yet Peter quotes this passage in the first Christian sermon spoken on Pentecost (Acts 2:14–26). He tells the crowd that this prophecy of Joel is fulfilled on that day, as the disciples were filled with the Holy Spirit and spoke the Gospel in languages they had not studied. We might also remember that the sun was darkened by day at Jesus' crucifixion (Matthew 27:45), and that people were raised from the dead when Jesus died (Matthew 27:52).

The next age (post-resurrection) has already begun. And yet it has not fully arrived. In a way, it's like dawn. Darkness fades as the sun begins to rise and, for about half an hour, it's almost light. This is sometimes called "false dawn." It seems like dawn; yet when the sun finally comes up, real dawn is so much brighter.

The New Testament age is a little like a "false dawn." The Son has arisen, the light shines, but the full light of the Son won't be evident until His glorious return. Many Old Testament prophetic passages that look forward to the coming of Messiah conceive of the first and second coming as though it were one event, which it is—the victory of Christ, crucified and risen!

## Notes to Chapter 9

1 Prophetesses include Miriam, Moses' sister (Exodus 15:20); Deborah, judge of Israel (Judges 4:4); Huldah (2 Kings 22:14); and Isaiah's wife (Isaiah 8:3).

2 Not every person who prophesies accurately is a believer. Sometimes a person prophesies because of the office he holds, as Caiaphas did in John 11:51. Caiaphas apparently did not believe in Jesus as his Savior. Yet he prophesied, because he held the office of high priest.

3 The four daughters of Philip the Evangelist prophesied (Acts 21:9) and the women of Corinth were permitted to prophesy as long as they covered their heads (1 Corinthians 11:2–16).

4 Not everyone knew that Jesus was born in Bethlehem. Since He came from Nazareth in Galilee, people thought He was born there. (See John 7:41–42.) Being from Nazareth was not a claim to fame (as Nathanael notes in John 1:46), but even this fulfills prophecy (as Matthew records in 2:23).

5 This event is presented in very vivid and picturesque language in Revelation 12:1–5.

6 Since a covenant was "cut" by sacrificing an animal at the time it took effect, it was sealed in blood. When Jesus institutes the Lord's Supper, He draws our attention to this by saying, "This cup is the new covenant in My blood" (1 Corinthians 11:25).

# Parables in the Bible

When we first learn the Bible, we often learn it by means of the stories our teachers tell us. Many of these stories are parables that Jesus told and which the Gospel writers wrote down. But parables can present a problem when we ask, "What is the intended meaning?" Unlike narrative sections of the Bible, symbolism frequently requires a reader to "decode" the story to discover the original, intended meaning.

What is a parable? Do we have any rules to help us understand them as the original storyteller intended? Why did Jesus tell parables in the first place?

## Definition of a Parable

Perhaps we best define a parable in simple terms: *A parable is an earthly story with a heavenly meaning.* Although we find a few parables in the Old Testament, most biblical parables occur in the New Testament, almost all of them in the gospels.

These parables are pictures of the kingdom of God in action, with some element of mystery. The heart of a parable is comparison, but a parable is more than a comparison. The difference between these two may be illustrated by looking at Deuteronomy 25:4 (cited by Paul in 1 Corinthians 9:9–10 and 1 Timothy 5:17–18) and contrasting it with the parable of the mustard seed (Mark 4:30–32).

In Deuteronomy 25:4 Moses writes, "Do not muzzle an ox while it is treading out the grain." On the surface, it seems that Moses is simply giving a humane command to people who use oxen to thresh grain.[1] However, the context (as we have seen so often) alerts us to the fact that this may not be so. The section of Deuteronomy in which 25:4 appears deals with people, not animals, particularly people who are in trouble.

Deuteronomy 25:1–3 prescribes flogging as a punishment, but humanely limits the number of lashes. Deuteronomy 25:5–10 records the Levirite law, a regulation that requires a near kinsman to raise up a child for a childless, deceased relative. This ensures the continuation of the family line.

Does Moses really have oxen in mind in verse 4, or could he be encouraging his readers to realize the need for humane treatment of people just as they humanely treat an ox while it is treading out the grain? When Paul cites this verse in 1 Corinthians and 1 Timothy, he uses it to support his position that a person has the right to make a living from preaching and teaching the Gospel. In 1 Corinthians 9:9–10 he asks, "Is it about oxen that God is concerned? Surely he says this for us, doesn't he?" By the word *thresh* Paul creates the comparison between the ox threshing and the man threshing. What do they have in common? Both hope to share the benefits of their work.

Sometimes Jesus tells long and elaborate stories (like the parable of the prodigal son in Luke 15:11–32). At other times His parables are quite short, as in the case of the parable of the mustard seed (Mark 4:30–32; Matthew 13:31–32; Luke 13:18–19). The kingdom of God, Jesus says, is like a mustard seed. It starts out very small and grows very large, so large that various kinds of birds can find shade in its branches.[2]

How is the mustard seed like the kingdom of God? Both start small and grow large over a long period of time. Jesus may have had a second point of comparison in mind if He was thinking of Daniel 4:21 when He spoke this parable. In the dream that Daniel interpreted a tree houses many kinds of birds. The tree represented a kingdom so large that it "extends to distant parts of the earth" (Daniel 4:22) and includes all kinds of people. If this is background for the parable, Jesus may be hinting that His kingdom would be open for people of all ethnic backgrounds—and not, as was often popularly thought, for Jewish people only.[3]

# Guidelines for Interpretation

We can offer a number of guidelines for interpreting parables:

1. A parable usually has one main point; any other points are secondary.
2. A parable illustrates, not establishes, doctrine. We do not use a parable to try to "prove" a doctrinal teaching.
3. A parable creates a comparison, but we should not compare every detail in every parable to something in the real world.
4. The details of a parable come from the real world. Impossible things (like talking dogs or flying pigs) do not appear in Jesus' parables. However, sometimes a parable includes an action that would be shocking and probably would never actually occur (as in the parable of the friend at midnight).
5. New Testament parables often have a real world background, either in the Old Testament or in the history of Palestine.

# The Reason for Parables

In Mark 4:10–12 (parallel passages are Matthew 13:14–15; Luke 8:10) Jesus explains the reason for parables. He has been conducting His public ministry for some time (perhaps a year or so) and opposition has begun to form (recorded in Mark 3). Thus Jesus turns to parables as a form of teaching. This prevents His enemies from interfering with His ministry of teaching, preaching, and healing. Parables are stories. How can His adversaries charge Him in ecclesiastical court (the Great Sanhedrin) or in secular court (Pontius Pilate) with telling stories?

Read Mark 4:10–12 and answer the following:

1. To whom has the "secret" (or "mystery") of the kingdom been given?
2. Which Old Testament passage does Jesus quote?
3. What is the original context of this Old Testament passage?
4. How long will the hardness of heart last in the original context?

By means of parables Jesus keeps His Messianic status a secret, revealing it only to His disciples. At the same time the parables both hide and reveal. They reveal spiritual truths to those in the kingdom of God— those who believe in Jesus—and hide them from those outside the kingdom—those who do not believe in Jesus. Unbelievers may understand that some of the parables are spoken against them (as in Mark 12:12), but can do very little about it.

Jesus cites Isaiah 6:9–10, part of Isaiah's call by God to be a prophet. God lets Isaiah know that the people will reject his message, ignore his warnings, and turn their backs on both God and His prophet. God will harden their hearts until the cities lie ruined, the houses are desolated, and the land is utterly forsaken (Isaiah 6:11). Then the people will cry to God for help. This prophecy was fulfilled within 20 years.

By citing Isaiah 6:9–10 Jesus reveals the reason for using parables in His teaching ministry. Also, He hints that He will continue to speak in parables until the judgment of God is executed—that is, until He dies on the cross for the sins of the world. His Messianic status and the true nature of the kingdom (faith in Jesus as God and Lord) remain hidden until after that time.[4] After the judgment of God has been executed upon Jesus, the news of the kingdom will be proclaimed beginning in Jerusalem, then Judea-Samaria, and even to the ends of the earth (as Jesus promises in Acts 1:8).

# Practice Interpreting Parables

We will read three parables: the parable of the sower (Mark 4:1–20), the parable of the prodigal son (Luke 15:11–32), and an Old Testament parable (2 Samuel 12:1–10).

## Mark 4:1–20

Read Mark 4:3–8 and answer the following:

1.  What is the main point of the parable?
2.  What is the background of the parable?
3.  What secondary points, if any, do you find in this parable?
4.  Which elements in the story represent something outside the story?

In a few parables, like this one, Jesus answers these questions (Mark 4:13–20).[5] The main point is that a person enters the kingdom of God and becomes fruitful by means of the Word. Those who reject the Word or lose it over a period of time are unfruitful. (No deeds of faith occur, because they lack or lose saving faith.) Jesus uses the agriculture of the day as the background of the parable. It is similar to our own methods in some ways and different in others. The farmer scattered the seed by hand on top of the soil and then plowed it under. Scholars debate whether the average farmer would have sown seed on ground he knew to be rocky or shallow.

By sowing seed over all the ground, the farmer in the parable sows most generously, almost excessively. (Perhaps this is a secondary point: Jesus sows the Word among all types of people.) For Jesus to make His point—the purpose of the story—seed must fall on various soils. Some who hear God's Word do not believe it, and they did not put it into practice in their lives.

In this parable (and in the others that Jesus explains), each element of the story represents something in the real world. The soil represents people, the birds of the air represent Satan, the seed is the Word, the sun symbolizes persecution or trouble, and thorns reflect the deceitfulness of wealth and the desire for material goods.

# Luke 15:11–32

We can easily interpret the parables Jesus explains. But what of the parables He does not explain?

In Luke 15 the author records a series of three parables. He gives us the context by recording the historical situation for these three (15:1–2). Jesus tells a parable of a man who loses and then finds one of 100 sheep. Next Jesus relates a parable of a woman who loses and then finds one of 10 coins.

Both parables contained elements that would have offended the Pharisees and their scribes (experts in Old Testament law). Shepherding was a lowly, sometimes despised profession (every shepherd worked on the Sabbath) and women were second-class citizens. Jesus boldly asks His audience to think of themselves as a shepherd and then to imagine themselves as a woman, both of which would have angered the Pharisees. Jesus explicitly tells us the point in both of these parables: God wants sinners to repent and turn to Him; when they do, He gladly forgives their sins. This sets up the reader of Luke's gospel for the third parable, a much longer story with a strong main point and a biting secondary question.

Read Luke 15:11–32 and answer the following:

1. What is the main point of the parable?
2. Why are the actions of the younger son so shocking?
3. What changes the younger son from a scheming and selfish person into someone who truly repents?
4. How does the older son reveal his attitude towards his father?
5. How does the father humiliate himself with both sons?

Jesus repeats the main point of the two preceding parables: God wants sinners to repent, and He gladly forgives them. Undoubtedly this simple point strikes home in the heart of Jesus' audience much more forcefully than it did in the first two parables, largely due to a series of shocking and surprising events.

First, the younger son asks for his inheritance. Culturally, this was never done. That would be like asking your father to drop dead. The father's response may have been equally shocking—he gives the boy his inheritance![6] Jesus' original audience might well have expected the father in the story to disown his son and expel him from house and village, but the father simply turns over the young man's inheritance to him.

Two big questions arise about the parable. First, what changes the selfish boy into a repentant son? Second, do all the parts of the story represent something outside of the story?

Your answer to the first question may depend to some extent on the Bible translation you are using. In the King James Version the boy asks the father in 15:21 exactly what he planned to ask him in 15:19. In more modern versions the son's request in 15:21 differs somewhat from what he planned to ask in 15:19. He does not ask his dad for a job. Older and more reliable copies of the Greek New Testament, discovered after the King James translation was made, do not include "make me like one of your hired men" in 15:21.[7]

The difference between verses 19 and 21 provides an opportunity to examine variations in reputable interpretations of the parable. Most traditional interpretations pretty much ignore the difference between the verses. They simply portray the son as a penitent sinner returning home.

Some Bible scholars (such as Ken Bailey, in *Finding the Lost: Cultural Keys to Luke 15*, CPH 1992) argue that the words in verse 19 ("make me like one of your hired men") indicate that the young man had not repented; he merely had concocted a scheme to get onto his father's payroll. In Bailey's view the young man's only interest was to play on his father's sympathies and get a job working for him (expecting much better pay and working conditions).[8] Only after the father runs to him (men of stature did not run in that society) and so warmly welcomes him back, does this young man finally repent, confessing his sin before his father without trying to get something out of him. Repentance, in this view, follows the Gospel (the demonstration of the father's love) rather than the Law (the decrepit condition in which the son found himself).

Regardless of the interpretation we choose, we see that the young man recognizes the wretchedness of his condition, and his father's love (a self-humiliating love!) leads him to recognize that he is a forgiven and accepted son and heir.

Moving to the second question, do all the parts of the story represent something outside of the story? That was true with the parable of the sower, but we shall find that it does not work with this parable (nor with some others), even though we sometimes try to make it work.

Given the context of Luke 15 (and the contrast between sinners and the Pharisees who considered themselves righteous),[9] we can readily see the younger son as a figure representing sinners and the older son as a character symbolizing the "righteous" Pharisees—indeed, any self-righteous person. However, we note limitations when we attempt to have the father represent God, since the story does not provide a complete picture of God. (For example, nobody dies for the sins of either son.) Regardless, the father represents a characteristic of God. God is the waiting, loving Father. He loves sinners and wants them to repent.

We dare not try to make all of the details of the story reflect some reality outside of the story. Doing so could make interpreting parables no more than an entertaining—but ultimately useless—game. What does the ring symbolize? What does the fatted calf represent? What is the "deeper meaning" of the robe or of the kiss or the fact that the father in the story put his arms around the young man's neck? What do the pigs symbolize and what symbolic value do the pods have? What is the real world meaning of the goat that the older son complains about? We could go on and on, and never get to the point that Jesus wants to make.

The younger son returns, repents, and is forgiven. His father celebrates by throwing a party, but the older brother refuses to come in. Again the father humiliates himself as he comes outside, leaving the party, to plead with his son.[10] And what happens to the older boy? Jesus leaves that to our imagination.

Jesus tells an open-ended parable that forcefully invites the Pharisees to join in the party—to rejoice with God and with His angels over the sinners that repent and are forgiven. Will they or won't they? At the time of the story, the question was still very much in doubt.

## 2 Samuel 12:1–10

In the third parable, an Old Testament story, we see again the importance of context. Read 2 Samuel 12:1–10 and answer the following:

1. What events lead up to this parable? (2 Kings 11)
2. Why does God send Nathan to David?
3. What was David's judgment against the rich man in Nathan's story?
4. What was the ultimate point of Nathan's parable?

The history of 2 Samuel 11 provides the background to the story in 2 Samuel 12. The author records that in the spring, when kings go off to war,[11] David stayed home in Jerusalem and General Joab led the Israelite army against the Ammonites. While home, David had an affair with the wife of one of Joab's soldier's, Uriah the Hittite.[12] In an effort to cover up the affair, David resorts to a number of ploys to get Uriah to sleep with his wife, Bathsheba. However, God's Law specifically required that a man on active military duty refrain from marital relations. Uriah, faithful to that Law, refused to sleep with his own wife. David, guilty of the capital crime of adultery,[13] conspires with his general, Joab, to have Uriah killed in battle. The problem is compounded when Joab arranges to have several soldiers killed so the murder isn't obvious.

God sends Nathan to confront David—to rebuke David for his crimes and to provide an opportunity for repentance. God intends to use the story recorded in 2 Samuel 12:1–4 to lead David to repentance. David pronounces the rich man guilty of a crime deserving death. However, since the Law does not allow that, David fines the rich man the price of the sheep times four.

Nathan sums up his point neatly in the direct address, "You are the man!" (2 Samuel 12:7).[14] By means of this parable David realizes that he has sinned against God and makes his confession (2 Samuel 12:13; see also Psalms 32 and 51).

To interpret this parable we need not figure out what the poor man represents, what the rich man symbolizes, what the rich man's guests stand for, and the significance of the ewe. The details of the parable do not line up with the specific details of David's actions. If the details of the parable corresponded to the details of history, the poor man in the parable would be murdered and the ewe lamb stolen by the rich man to be added to his already impressive flock.

It is important that we recognize that parables generally have one main point. Sometimes the details of parables are symbolic (like the parable of the sower). But most of the time, as with Nathan's parable, they are not. Nathan's story in chapter 12 has one thing in common with David's history in chapter 11: a man who had much violated the rights of a man who had little, taking what was another man's for his own.

# Final Guidelines

What have we learned in our practice session of interpreting parables?

1. Context is important; always read the material before and after the unit under study.
2. Understanding the background of the parables is helpful. Culture, history, geography, and the like differ markedly from our own.
3. Sometimes we need to use various tools for Bible study in order to "get the point." (These tools will be listed in chapter 12.)

# Notes to Chapter 10

1 A good Bible encyclopedia will help the modern city dweller understand this ancient agricultural practice. Chapter 12 will discuss various tools for Bible study, including an encyclopedia.

2 This is an example of the classic argument "from the lesser to the greater." If something is true in the case of a lesser thing, how much more true is it in the case of a greater thing!

3 Based on Malachi 3:1, which predicts Messiah to appear suddenly in the temple, most people expected the Messianic kingdom to come rapidly once the Messiah publicly declared Himself. The parable of the mustard seed is a strong contrast to this popular expectation.

4 Jesus anticipates this in Matthew 10:27 and specifically commands silence regarding His Messianic kingship in Matthew 16:20 and 17:9.

5 Other parables where Jesus explains the meaning of the story include the parable of the net (Matthew 13:47–52) and the parable of the weeds (Matthew 13:24–30, 36–43).

6 The younger son got 1/3 of the inheritance; the older brother got 2/3. The law of primogeniture (the law of the "first born") was that he receive a double portion of the inheritance (Deuteronomy 21:17). Daughters would receive an inheritance if a man had no son (Numbers 25:7–8).

7 How our English Bible came to us will be the subject of part 3 in this book, "How We Got the Bible."

8 After all, how low could a Jewish boy go? He was feeding the pigs of Gentiles.

9 Remember that "righteous" describes a person who keeps his end of the bargain— in this case, God's Law.

10 This would have been most shocking to Jesus' original listeners.

11 Spring was the beginning of the warm, dry season. It is not clear why David remained at the palace instead of leading his army.

12 Note the irony in the fact that the foreigner, Uriah, is ultimately faithful to the covenant, while the covenant king, David, a man after God's own heart (as he is called in 1 Samuel 13:14 and Acts 13:22), proves unfaithful.

13 Adultery, that is, having intercourse with another man's wife, is a specific crime that God forbids in Leviticus 20:10 and Deuteronomy 22:22. The Law punished this sin by the execution of both parties.

14 Usually kings in the Near East could not be approached so casually. For example, Esther takes her life in her hands when she speaks to the king of Persia, her husband, without first being invited to do so. The king of God's people, bound by the covenant, is here held accountable to his King, the Lord, for what he has done.

# Apocalyptic Writing

The term *apocalyptic* comes from a Greek word that means *unveiled; revealed.* Imagine the day of dedication for a new statue in a town park. A large cover is draped over the figure. As the crowd gathers in anticipation, the covering is slowly lifted. The base, the middle, then the whole statue is revealed. That's what "apocalyptic" writings do. They lift the veil from the future so that everyone can see clearly what lies ahead.

It may seem ironical that apocalyptic writings almost always use codes: numbers are symbolic, colors have meaning, and powerful visions of very strange creatures abound. We began our study of interpretation by stating that we need to stick to the plain meaning of the text. In apocalyptic writings we replace that principle with a different guide: **Know the code!**

## Apocalyptic Writing in the Ancient World

Apocalyptic writings were quite common in the ancient world, particularly from the second century before Jesus through the second century after His death and resurrection. Quite a number of non-Scriptural apocalyptic books were written during these four centuries: *1 Enoch, 2 Baruch, 4 Ezra* (also known as *2 Esdras*), *3 Baruch, Apocalypse of Abraham,* and others.

Perhaps you have never heard of these books, much less read them. Scripture never mentions and rarely quotes these apocalypses. In the book of Jude the author quotes 1 Enoch 1:9 (in verses 14–15) and reflects the Assumption of Moses in verse 9.

Quotations of works outside the Bible are not limited to apocalypses. In Titus 1:12 Paul quotes Epimenides, in Acts 17:18 he cites Aratus, and in 2 Peter 2:22 Peter cites a proverb popularized in the ancient story of Ahikar. Thus, when Jude cites a book outside of the Bible with which his readers would have been familiar, he is following in the footsteps of Peter and Paul.

# Apocalyptic Writing in the Bible

The longest apocalyptic part of the Bible is the Revelation of Jesus Christ to John. Strictly speaking, Revelation is not an apocalypse but a prophecy that uses apocalyptic imagery. Revelation lacks a number of features common to true apocalypses. (For example, the author does not claim to be a great figure from the past, such as Enoch or Moses, but identifies himself as John.) John calls his book a *prophecy* (Revelation 1:3; 10:11; 22:7, 10). He then proceeds to reveal the events of the New Testament era, culminating in the final judgment and in the advent of the new heaven and new earth.

John's message, like the message of other apocalyptic prophecies of the Bible, assures us that Jesus conquers Satan in the end. No matter what persecution a Christian faces, we must remain faithful to Jesus because He (and only He) will give the crown of life to the one who faithfully endures persecution (as He promises in Revelation 2:10).

We also find apocalyptic prophecies in Joel, Ezekiel, Zechariah (chapters 9–14), Isaiah (chapters 24–27), and Daniel (chapters 7–12). Some writers call the parts of the gospels where Jesus talks about the destruction of Jerusalem and the end of the world apocalyptic, or the "little apocalypse" (Matthew 24–25, Mark 13, Luke 21). Since we try to base our doctrine on clear, unambiguous passages of Scripture, we usually do not base our teachings on apocalyptic sections. These portions of Scripture tend to play a supportive rather than a foundational role in establishing our teachings.

# Guidelines for Understanding Apocalyptic Writing

When we do read apocalyptic sections, three things are very helpful:

**1. Keep the clear parts of Scripture in view.** Like ancient sailors who keep the coastline in view, we do well to have "control chapters" so we don't get lost in apocalyptic. For Revelation, it's a good idea to keep Matthew 24–25 in our mind's eye.

**2. Understand the outline.** Know how the smaller parts fit together to make up the whole. In Revelation, for example, we have an introduction (chapter 1) and a conclusion (20:11–22:21) with seven units between them. Several of these units overlap (the six seals, 6:1–8:5; the six trumpets, 8:6–11:19; and the six bowls, 15:1–16:21) and describe the same period of time but with a growing emphasis on the end of time. Some people take each section as referring to a successive period of time and thus misunderstand John's point.

**3. Know the code.** Colors and numbers have meaning.[1] Red and black are generally bad; white is good. Three denotes God and four refers to creation. Seven equals fullness and ten indicates completeness. Thus, 144,000 dressed in white (Revelation 7 and 14) equals the complete number of people who are saved by grace through faith in Jesus Christ. Their sins are forgiven and they are credited with Jesus' good works (thus, they wear white) and not one believer is missing. God's people (3 x 4 = 12) from both Old and New Testament times (12 x 12 = 144), the complete number God has saved by faith (10 cubed = 1,000) are represented by the number 144,000 (144 x 1,000).[2] Using numbers in this way seems strange to us, but it does not take long to grasp John's meaning once we know the code.

Remember, though, that not all numbers in the Bible are symbolic. For example, the number 153 has no hidden meaning when

Peter catches 153 fish (John 21:11). He simply caught a large number of sizable fish.

One could compare this with playing various card games with the same deck of cards. We could play rummy or we could play solitaire with the same deck but with different rules. So it is with different types of literature—straightforward historical sections call for sticking with the plain and obvious meaning of the text. Apocalyptic prophecies require a slightly different set of rules that take into consideration the codes the author uses.

# Practicing the Guidelines

Let's read Revelation 20:1–3 and answer the following questions:

1. Who is the angel in 20:1?
2. What might the chain in 20:1 represent?
3. Who is the dragon in 20:2?
4. How long is the dragon chained?
5. For what purpose is the dragon chained?

Normally we think of angels as spirit-beings without bodies, although they can take physical forms when it pleases God.[3] The world *angel* means *messenger.* It can sometimes refer to people (as it does in Luke 7:24).

Given the description in Revelation 10 and also here in Revelation 20, the angel might well be Jesus. The picture of the angel in 20:1 is consistent with Jesus. He descended from heaven in the incarnation, possesses the keys of the kingdom of God (Matthew 16:19), and the power to cast demons into hell (Luke 8:31, which uses the same word for hell—*abyss*). Jesus is also the one who told the parable of the stronger man binding the strong man and then ransacking the strong man's house. We normally take this figure of speech to refer to Jesus overthrowing Satan's reign on earth and saving sinners from Satan's bondage (Luke 11:21–22).

If this identification is correct (that the angel of 20:1 is Jesus), then the chain might symbolize the Holy Spirit. The church was "born" on Pentecost with the outpouring of the Holy Spirit (Acts 2), and Paul talks about a restraining force on Satan (2 Thessalonians 2:6–7) during the New Testament age.[4] Further, Jesus talks of the Father sending Him and, in His name, sending the Spirit. This interpretation seems to be supported by the fact in Scripture that only God Himself is more powerful than Satan. Even the archangel Michael refers Satan to God rather than rebuking Satan himself (Jude 9).

Our answer to the first two questions may seem a bit tenuous, but we find that we cannot easily make hard and fast, solid identification of apocalyptic images. The better you know the rest of Scripture, the more readily you can identify apocalyptic figures.

The third question is much easier. The figure of a dragon appears for the first time in Revelation 12:3 and occurs a total of 12 times in the book. This character cannot be anyone but the chief of the fallen angels.

The text says that he is chained for a thousand years. But how long is that? Numbers in Revelation are consistently symbolic, and that is the case here. One thousand represents the complete time God has set aside for the Gentile mission, that is, for Gospel outreach to the nations (Matthew 24:14); 10 cubed = 1,000, a symbol for the New Testament era.

Some object to this interpretation. They maintain that, since evil still seems to be present in the world, it is impossible to think that Satan is bound. Therefore, they say, this 1,000 years must refer to a literal reign of Jesus before Judgment Day. As we read all of verse 2, however, we find that John does not say Satan is bound so that he cannot do anything at all. Rather, John says that Satan is bound so that he cannot deceive the nations (the Gentiles) anymore. In other words, Satan cannot stop the Gospel's success.

The story of Jesus and His crucifixion and resurrection will go out from Jerusalem to the four corners of the earth and people will be brought into the kingdom of God's grace. Satan, try as he might, cannot stop this. Spreading this Gospel news is the purpose of the New Testament era and the job description of the church. Jesus promises that not even the gates of

Hades will prevail against the church in her mission (Matthew 16:18). At the end of the New Testament age Satan will be released for a short time, and then the end of the world will come.

This same message of hope and confidence appears in Revelation 11. There two witnesses (representing the church)[5] evangelize for 1,260 days—3 1/2 years—and cannot be harmed.[6] After their time of witness ends, they are killed, and their bodies lie in the street for 3 1/2 days, after which they stand up and the judgment of the world commences.[7]

Several things become quickly apparent as we interpret apocalyptic writing:

- The better we know the rest of Scripture, the better we are able to interpret apocalyptic prophecies in the Bible.
- The better we know the apocalyptic prophecy, the more likely we are to understand a particular passage or paragraph as the author intended it.
- As exciting as it might be to attempt to interpret Revelation, it is better to begin a lifetime of Bible study elsewhere. We need to learn to walk before trying to run. If we begin our study with apocalyptic prophecy, we may frequently read our own ideas into the text (a very popular game) and make believe that the original writer had our thoughts in mind.

## Notes to Chapter 11

1 A good resource for this is Bruce M. Metzger, *Breaking the Code: Understanding the Book of Revelation* (Nashville: Abingdon Press, 1993).

2 It is very important that your Bible translate the numbers as they appear in Revelation rather than convert them to modern equivalents. Revelation 14:20 speaks of 1,600 stadia, a Roman unit of distance. If a translation uses a number other than 1,600 when converting to a modern equivalent (e.g., "about 200 miles"), it loses part of John's message. That message is contained in the number 1,600, not in the distance. 1,600 = all of creation (4 x 4 x 10 x 10).

3 Sometimes these forms are human, as in the resurrection and ascension accounts, and sometimes they are quite bizarre, as in Revelation 4 and Ezekiel 1.

4 Greek nouns have gender (masculine, feminine, neuter) like German and many

other languages. The gender of the restraining force in 2 Thessalonians 2:6 is neuter, and the gender of the restraining force in 2 Thessalonians 2:7 is masculine. The word Spirit in Greek is neuter, and yet the Holy Spirit is a person in the Trinity. The alternation between neuter and masculine might reflect this, or the one who restrains might refer to Jesus in verse 7.

5   Strong echoes from Zechariah and Ezekiel show up in Revelation 11.

6   Like Elijah in 1 Kings 17, they stop the rain. In 2 Kings 1, fire consumes their enemies.

7   This is very similar to material in Daniel, especially chapters 7 and 12. Metzger, *Breaking the Code* (p. 13), points out that of the 404 verses in Revelation, 278 contain one or more references to the Old Testament.

# Bible Tools for Better Bible Study

When we pick up our Bibles, we begin an adventure. When we open our Bibles, we open the door to a world very different from our own in many ways.

Human nature has not changed since Adam and Eve rebelled against God in Genesis 3, but almost everything else about the people and places in the Bible is different from our world. Each of the books of the Bible was written by a real person (or, in some cases, people). That person lived and died in a specific culture and a particular geography with a history and a language that seem quite strange to us today. Yet God inspired these authors, moving them to write these books—for our salvation.[1]

On the one hand, the basic message of Scripture is simple: "Believe in the Lord Jesus Christ and you will be saved" (Acts 16:31). On the other hand, much of what God says to us can be lost through ignorance of the original language and historical context. What tools can help us as we begin the adventure of Bible study?

## The Original Languages

As we will see in the next chapter, the Bible was originally written in three languages: Hebrew, Aramaic,[2] and Greek. The Aramaic portions are quite small (some of Ezra and several chapters in Daniel), so that most who study the original languages study only Hebrew and Greek.

These original languages are the inspired text of Scripture. Our English translations, however, are quite good. Bible students who do not work with the original languages can be quite confident that they have an accurate rendition of the text.

Nonetheless, most people who have the time and self-discipline can learn the biblical languages. Since learning any language is much easier with a teacher, a Bible student who can travel to a seminary may wish to check whether the seminary offers language instruction to interested parties.

Though not as effective as class instruction for most, a computer program also can provide language instruction. Instruction in both Hebrew and Greek is available. For example, Parsons Technology (P.O. Box 100, Hiawatha, Iowa 52233-0100) has tutorials for both languages on CD-ROM for about $40 each. Also, a number of text and workbook courses are available.[3]

God's Word is effective whether in the original language or in translation. We can compare the difference between knowing the original language and a translation with two television sets—one a 12" black-and-white model with rabbit ears and the other a 60" color big-screen set with excellent cable reception. The detail and color are much better on the bigger TV, but you get the same plot line and characters on both sets.

Whether you study the Bible in the original languages or in translation, the same God reveals our sin and our Savior, Jesus Christ. A Bible student who works exclusively with translations may purchase an edition of the Bible that puts various translations in parallel columns. (We will discuss various modern translations in chapter 16.)

# Concordances

A concordance lists the Bible passages in which a particular word appears. A complete concordance—which lists all the passages in which the word appears—is available in large books or computer programs. Many

Bibles contain smaller concordances, such as the one in the *Concordia Self-Study Bible* (found in the pages just before the maps), that list only selected passages.

Obviously, a concordance becomes a very helpful tool for word studies. However, one needs to be aware that a single Hebrew or Greek term can be translated by a variety of English terms. Therefore the word study in translations may not yield the same results as word studies in the original languages. Furthermore, each translation might use a different English word to translate the same original term so that the translations seem to disagree with each other.

For example, the Greek word *sōzein* can be translated *to save* in the sense of "to rescue from God's wrath on Judgment Day." It also can be translated *to be healed; made well* in the sense of being saved from a disease. In Mark 6:56 the evangelist records that Jesus was in Gennesaret and that sick people touched His garment and "were healed" (NIV, NRSV). However, the NKJV translates this "made well." If you are doing a concordance search you might have a difficult time finding all the passages that speak of Jesus healing people, unless you know all the ways in which the Greek word *sōzein* is translated in that particular version. The problem is compounded by the fact that not only can one Hebrew or Greek word be translated by a variety of English terms, but one English word can be used to translate several different Hebrew or Greek terms.

Still, a concordance is a valuable tool for Bible study. It keeps the student in the Bible itself rather than giving opinions about the Bible (primary versus secondary research). *Strong's Exhaustive Concordance* and *Young's Analytical Concordance* are both excellent Bible tools (KJV). Computer concordances are even more impressive, easier to use (once the student becomes familiar with them), but far more expensive. Logos software produces a variety of editions of its software and the Bible Works for Windows by Hermeneutika is very useful. These software programs offer a multitude of features not found in books. A student who considers buying one of these should consider carefully which features in the software are really needed.

# Bible Dictionaries and Encyclopedias

Bible dictionaries are usually one-volume books, and encyclopedias may come as multivolume sets. A dictionary lists words found in the Bible (including proper names) and gives a thumbnail sketch for that entry. A Bible dictionary is a handy tool for gathering all the pertinent data about a particular topic in the Bible. *The New Unger's Bible Dictionary* and *Easton's Bible Dictionary* are both popular. (Unger also is responsible for a popular handbook to the Bible.) The following example from *Easton's Bible Dictionary* shows what a Bible dictionary does. This example comes as part of Bible Works for Windows. The following information appears under the entry "Abishag":

> Father of (i.e., "given to") error, a young woman of Shunem, distinguished for her beauty. She was chosen to minister to David in his old age. She became his wife (1 Kings 1:3,4,15). After David's death Adonijah persuaded Bathsheba, Solomon's mother, to entreat the king to permit him to marry Abishag. Solomon suspected in this request an aspiration to the throne, and therefore caused him to be put to death (1Ki 2:17–25).

For comparison, *Nave's Topical Dictionary* (also part of the Bible Works for Windows software) has a much shorter entry under "Abishag":

> Wife of David (1 Ki 1:1–4 2:13–25)

A Bible encyclopedia is generally longer (three to five volumes) and includes more pictures. It may have more topics than a dictionary and may cover broader topics (e.g., "marriage" covers pages 92-102 of volume 4 in the Zondervan *Pictorial Encyclopedia of the Bible*). Bible dictionaries and encyclopedias are very helpful tools for Bible study. They help the student get an overview of a particular subject as well as helping the student learn background information.

# Commentaries

A commentary is a verse-by-verse interpretation and explanation of Scripture. There are some one-volume commentaries. By virtue of their size, they are able to offer only limited comments (if any) on a particular Bible passage. Concordia Publishing House offers its *Self-Study Commentary,* and several others are on the market.

More thorough commentaries limit themselves to one or two books of the Bible at a time. Most commentary series are designed for pastors and Bible teachers, but (thankfully) a number are available for the lay student. The *People's Bible Commentary* (CPH) is a series of paperback commentaries that provide a valuable source of help for the average and beginning Bible student.

# Study Bibles

Probably a good study Bible will get more use than the rest of these tools combined. However, a word of caution is in order. All study Bibles reflect the doctrine of their editors and publishers. Therefore it is important to choose a study Bible that is doctrinally dependable. For example, the *Concordia Self-Study Bible* contains introductory material, helpful footnotes, outlines, charts, graphs, and a limited concordance. Some study Bibles, such as the Scofield and Ryrie study Bibles, reflect millienialist beliefs. (Chapter 11 showed how this grows out of an erroneous interpretation of apocalyptic writing.)

# Other Books

Several other Bible aids may prove useful. These include *Chronological and Background Charts of the Old Testament* and *Chronological and Background Charts of the New Testament,* by Academie Books. Both are very useful, putting much information at the student's fingertips. Everett Ferguson's *Backgrounds of Early Christianity* (Grand Rapids: Eerdmans, 1993) provides some of the best background about the New Testament world. In addition to all these resources, new books and software become available on a regular basis. Check your bookstore (real or virtual) every so often to see what new tools are available.

# A Note of Caution

Every Bible tool (except for concordances) reflects the theology and outlook of the people who produced them. Take the time, if possible, to find out something about the author, editor, or publisher of a particular book. We need to be careful not to believe everything we read. The Bible itself is the only real authority; everything else is merely opinion.

As we have worked through several passages in parts 1 and 2 of this book, we have used various Bible tools to interpret particular passages. Sometimes the Bible passage under study required working with the original language. A beginning student of the Bible should not feel intimidated by problems that require more expertise than the student has, but should be willing to ask for help when it is needed. Pastors and other experienced Bible teachers do not know all the answers, but they can often steer the beginner in the right direction. Remember, though, that only the Bible is the authority; everything else is opinion.

## Notes to Chapter 12

1 Paul makes this point in 1 Corinthians 10:1–13 when he talks about the lesson we must learn from the Hebrews during the Exodus.

2 Aramaic looks like Hebrew in modern editions of the Hebrew Scriptures. At the risk of oversimplification, Aramaic is to Hebrew as German is to English—similar in appearance, but different languages nonetheless.

3 You can visit your local Christian bookstore, contact one of the mail-order book stores (such as Christian Book Distributors in Peabody, Massachusetts, http://chrbook.com), or visit an online book store (e.g., http://www.amazon.com).

# Part Three

## How We Got the Bible

The Bible is a library of many books written primarily in Hebrew and Greek over several centuries. Each of the two major parts, the Old Testament and the New Testament, contains different categories of books, such as history, poetry, and prophecy. Chapters 13 and 14 explore the Old Testament and the New Testament.

If you cannot read the languages in which the Bible was originally written, you will read the Bible in a translation or a paraphrase. This is the topic of chapter 15.

Some ancient books and writings outside the Bible help us understand the messages of Scripture. In chapter 16 you will learn about some of those writings.

**Old Testament**
# CHRONOLOGY

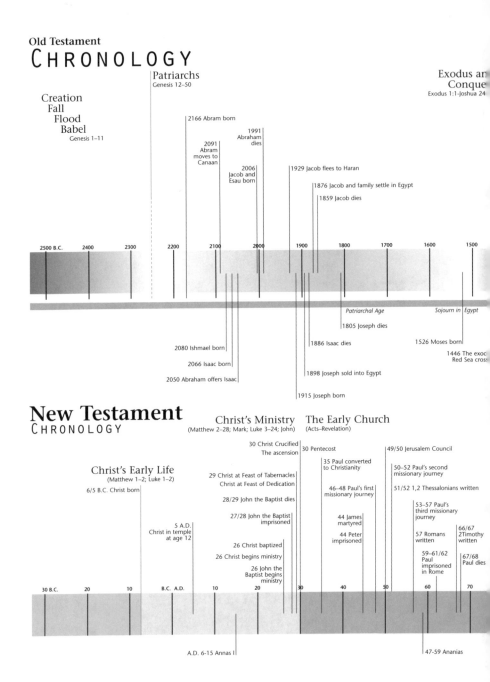

Patriarchs
Genesis 12–50

Creation
Fall
Flood
Babel
Genesis 1–11

Exodus an
Conque
Exodus 1:1-Joshua 24

2166 Abram born

1991
Abraham
dies

2091
Abram
moves to
Canaan

2006
Jacob and
Esau born

1929 Jacob flees to Haran

1876 Jacob and family settle in Egypt

1859 Jacob dies

| 2500 B.C. | 2400 | 2300 | 2200 | 2100 | 2000 | 1900 | 1800 | 1700 | 1600 | 1500 |

Patriarchal Age

Sojourn in Egypt

1805 Joseph dies

2080 Ishmael born

1886 Isaac dies

1526 Moses born

1446 The exod
Red Sea cross

2066 Isaac born

1898 Joseph sold into Egypt

2050 Abraham offers Isaac

1915 Joseph born

# New Testament
## CHRONOLOGY

Christ's Ministry
(Matthew 2–28; Mark; Luke 3–24; John)

The Early Church
(Acts–Revelation)

30 Christ Crucified
The ascension

30 Pentecost

49/50 Jerusalem Council

35 Paul converted
to Christianity

50–52 Paul's second
missionary journey

Christ's Early Life
(Matthew 1–2; Luke 1–2)

29 Christ at Feast of Tabernacles
Christ at Feast of Dedication

46–48 Paul's first
missionary journey

51/52 1,2 Thessalonians written

6/5 B.C. Christ born

28/29 John the Baptist dies

53–57 Paul's
third missionary
journey

5 A.D.
Christ in temple
at age 12

27/28 John the Baptist
imprisoned

44 James
martyred

66/67
2Timothy
written

57 Romans
written

26 Christ baptized

44 Peter
imprisoned

59–61/62
Paul
imprisoned
in Rome

67/68
Paul dies

26 Christ begins ministry

26 John the
Baptist begins
ministry

| 30 B.C. | 20 | 10 | B.C. A.D. | 10 | 20 | 30 | 40 | 50 | 60 | 70 |

A.D. 6-15 Annas I

47-59 Ananias

102

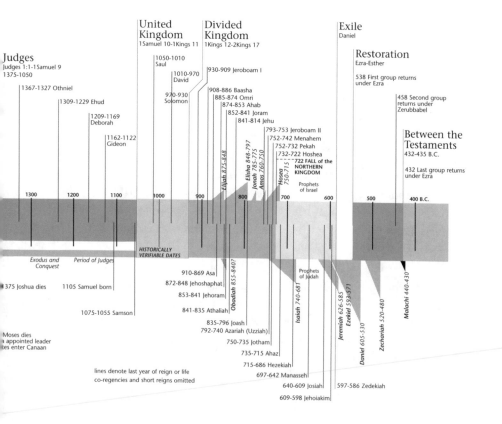

**Judges**
Judges 1:1-1Samuel 9
1375-1050

**United Kingdom**
1Samuel 10-1Kings 11

**Divided Kingdom**
1Kings 12-2Kings 17

**Exile**
Daniel

**Restoration**
Ezra-Esther

1367-1327 Othniel

1309-1229 Ehud

1209-1169 Deborah

1162-1122 Gideon

1050-1010 Saul

1010-970 David

970-930 Solomon

930-909 Jeroboam I

908-886 Baasha
885-874 Omri
874-853 Ahab
852-841 Joram
841-814 Jehu

793-753 Jeroboam II
752-742 Menahem
752-732 Pekah
732-722 Hoshea
722 FALL of the NORTHERN KINGDOM
Prophets of Israel

538 First group returns under Ezra

458 Second group returns under Zerubbabel

**Between the Testaments**
432-435 B.C.

432 Last group returns under Ezra

Elijah 875-848
Elisha 848-797
Jonah 785-775
Amos 760-750
Hosea 750-715

| 1300 | 1200 | 1100 | 1000 | 900 | 800 | 700 | 600 | 500 | 400 B.C. |

*HISTORICALLY VERIFIABLE DATES*

*Exodus and Conquest*  *Period of Judges*

1375 Joshua dies  1105 Samuel born

Prophets of Judah

Moses dies
a appointed leader
tes enter Canaan

910-869 Asa
872-848 Jehoshaphat
853-841 Jehoram
841-835 Athaliah

1075-1055 Samson

Obadiah 855-840?

835-796 Joash
792-740 Azariah (Uzziah)
750-735 Jotham
735-715 Ahaz
715-686 Hezekiah
697-642 Manasseh
640-609 Josiah
609-598 Jehoiakim

Isaiah 740-681

Jeremiah 626-585
Ezekiel 593-571

Daniel 605-530

Zechariah 520-480

Malachi 440-430

lines denote last year of reign or life
co-regencies and short reigns omitted

597-586 Zedekiah

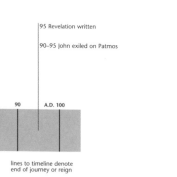

95 Revelation written

90–95 John exiled on Patmos

| 90 | A.D. 100 |

lines to timeline denote
end of journey or reign

Dates are approximate.
They depend on the interpretive
theories of various scholars.

# The Old Testament

We do not know exactly when writing was first invented. The oldest writing samples that still exist today date from around 3100 B.C. They come from Sumeria, a land between the Tigris and Euphrates rivers in modern Iraq. Egyptian writings from about the same time have also survived.

Our earliest Hebrew writing is a school boy's writing exercises from the tenth century B.C. This student used a clay tablet to list the months of the year and their agricultural significance. It was found in the town of Gezer and is known as the *Gezer calendar.* Several other archaeological finds have produced examples of Hebrew writing from the eighth century B.C. onwards.[1]

The earliest copy of the Hebrew Scriptures, however, was written much later. Until the discovery of the Dead Sea Scrolls in 1947, the oldest copy of the entire Old Testament in Hebrew that survived had been produced about A.D. 1000. The Dead Sea Scrolls included a large number of Hebrew Scriptures, about 95 percent of which matched the Hebrew Old Testament as we have it today. These Hebrew Scriptures must have been written down no later than the first century A.D., getting us almost 1,000 years closer than before to the originals.

# Authors and Date of Writing

The debate over who wrote the books of the Old Testament and when they were written has raged for over two centuries. While tradition plays a role in answering these questions, Scripture itself makes certain claims about authorship and date.

We will examine the first five books of the Bible, sometimes called the Pentateuch. According to several passages (Exodus 24:4; 34:28; Deuteronomy 4:13; 5:22; 10:4; and others) Moses wrote at least part of the Pentateuch. Referring to Deuteronomy 24:1–4, Jesus states that Moses wrote this section of Scripture (Mark 10:5; a parallel is Matthew 19:8). When the Sadducees refer to the levirate marriage law as having come from Moses (Mark 12:19; parallels are Matthew 22:24; Luke 20:28), Jesus does not correct them.

The internal testimony of Scripture clearly shows that Moses wrote at least some of the first five books of the Bible. Some parts may have been updated later (see Genesis 14:14; 36:31; 47:11), and the last chapter of Deuteronomy, which records Moses' death, may have been added by someone else. However, it is fair to say that as far as the record of Scripture is concerned, Moses is the author of the Pentateuch. Since the Exodus may be dated to 1446 B.C. (see 1 Kings 6:1), this would mean the first five books of the Bible were written in the last half of the 15th century B.C.[2] The events that took place prior to Moses' birth in Exodus 1 would have come down to Moses, most probably in oral form. However, some written records, especially from the time of Abraham (about 1900 B.C.), could have been part of the resources available to Moses. (At least five different writing systems were available to Abraham. He may well have been familiar with at least one of them.)

It might seem to us that oral transmission is not very reliable. However, people who cannot read or write—or who do very little reading or writing—depend on their memories much more than we do. The human mind is capable of memorizing a large amount of information without writing of any kind, as any child under the age of five demonstrates. Further, the first 11 chapters of Genesis seem to be designed to be memorized for later repetition. Certain patterns of speech, narrative organization, and even word counts can ensure that the story is remembered and passed on exactly as received. Hence, the task for Moses is very realistic, even without considering divine revelation.

Thus, Moses received both oral and written accounts of the events recorded in Genesis 1–Exodus 1. He included these accounts in his history of the Exodus and the Sinai wanderings, writing the books of Genesis through Deuteronomy. After the death of Moses, Joshua[3] (or someone else) recorded Deuteronomy 34.

Over the next one thousand years the Holy Spirit moved people to write down the history of Israel, the poetry of its musicians, the proverbs of its wise men, and the Law and Gospel of its prophets.

The Israelites divided their Bible into three sections: the Law (*Torah,* the five books of Moses), the Prophets, and the Writings. The Prophets were divided into history (the Former Prophets—Joshua through 2 Kings) and prophecy (the Latter Prophets—Isaiah through Malachi). The books of 1 and 2 Chronicles were included in the category "Writings." These were the last books of the Hebrew canon (the list of books that are accepted as Holy Scripture).

Some of the books of the Old Testament name their authors (e.g., most of the prophetic books) while others are anonymous (e.g., the books of Samuel and Kings). Some books are compilations of many writers (e.g., Psalms, Proverbs) and other books name their author by a kind of "pen name" (e.g., the author of Ecclesiastes is identified as *Qoheleth,* "the preacher").

Some dates are very easy to fix because of historical references contained in them (e.g., the visions of Ezekiel can usually be dated with certainty to the month, day, and year) while we cannot even determine the century in which others were written (e.g., Job). We can say, though, that over the period from the 15th century B.C. through the 4th century B.C. a variety of people wrote prose and poetry, prophecies and wisdom. God's people recognized these writings as special. They preserved them, read and studied them, and even died for them.

# The Old Testament in the New Testament

Jesus held the Old Testament in very high regard. His use of it shows how highly He thought of the Hebrew Scriptures. When Jesus faced Satan in the wilderness, He used Scripture to fight him. Jesus quoted from the part of the Old Testament that records the temptations Israel faced during 40 years in the wilderness. As Jesus finished His 40 days in the wilderness, He cited Deuteronomy 8:3; 6:16, 13 (see Matthew 4:1–11; a parallel is Luke 4:1–13).

Later, in Matthew 16:4, Jesus refers to the prophet Jonah, an apparent reference to His own coming death, burial, and resurrection. In Matthew 19:3–12 He refers to Genesis 1:27 and 2:24, all in reference to an issue raised by the Pharisees in light of Deuteronomy 24:1–4. Jesus cites Psalm 8:2 in defense of the children's praise at His triumphal entry into Jerusalem (Matthew 21:16). When Jesus quotes the first verse of Psalm 110 during the last week of His earthly ministry (Matthew 22:44), He says the Holy Spirit inspired David to write the psalm. Even in His most extreme suffering on the cross, Jesus quotes Scripture. Both Matthew and Mark record the fact that Jesus cites Psalm 22:1, a psalm of the righteous sufferer, during the crucifixion (Matthew 27:46; Mark 15:34).

The authors of the New Testament have the same high regard for the Old Testament as does Jesus. Even though Jesus and the New Testament writers often quote from the Greek translation of the Hebrew Scriptures (known as the Septuagint), they treat these Scriptures as the authoritative, inspired Word of God.[4] This is very helpful for us, because it confirms the fact that the Word of God is not bound to the original languages, but remains the Word of God even in translation.

# The Old Testament Canon

As stated earlier in this chapter, the canon is the list of books that are accepted as Holy Scripture. The Old Testament canon was fairly well fixed by the time of the New Testament (the first century A.D.). The last time the Hebrew canon was discussed seems to be the Council of Jamnia (or Yavneh) in A.D. 90.

At this gathering the status of several books was discussed, including the Song of Songs and Ecclesiastes. These books had apparently been considered Scripture for some time, but various features about each of these works may have troubled some rabbis. Some discussion over a few books continued in Jewish tradition. It seems, though, that by the first century A.D. the 39 books of the Old Testament were well established as Holy Scripture and had been considered such for some time.

# Summary and Conclusions

The writing of the Old Testament took place over about one thousand years. We cannot determine how many authors were involved. The time span covered in the Old Testament books ranges from the beginning of the world through the beginning of the fourth century B.C. As far as we know, none of the originals of any of the books has survived. The Dead Sea Scrolls contain some copies of the Hebrew Scriptures that date to the first and second centuries B.C.

Jesus and the authors of the New Testament regarded the Hebrew Scriptures as God's Word and understood that these Scriptures were written for our learning (Romans 15:4). The Old Testament is much longer than the New Testament. It includes a great deal of genealogies, history, geography, and regulations about the temple and ancient Jewish worship. Yet the Old Testament continues to point to Jesus Christ (John 5:39).

# Notes to Chapter 13

1   These include the Siloam Inscription, describing the completion of a tunnel in Jerusalem from about 705 B.C. and the Lachish Letters, communiqués from Lachish to Jerusalem from about 587 B.C. For a more complete listing of ancient texts relating to the Old Testament, see page 5 of the *Concordia Self-Study Bible.*

2   Many scholars argue that the Exodus took place in the 13th century B.C. However, the more conservative and traditional date of the 15th century B.C. still has a large number of defenders.

3   We know that Joshua could write because we know he wrote in public on at least two occasions (Joshua 8:32 and 24:26).

4   This is true even when the Septuagint is a little different from the Hebrew text. A good example is Genesis 2:24, which is cited four times in the New Testament (Matthew 19:5; Mark 10:8; 1 Corinthians 6:16; and Ephesians 5:31). The Hebrew text of Genesis 2:24 reads "*they* shall become one flesh" whereas the Septuagint reads "*the two* shall become one flesh."

# The New Testament

The New Testament is a much shorter collection of books and took considerably less time than the Old Testament to write. The earliest New Testament work,[1] either 1 Thessalonians or Galatians, was written about A.D. 50. The last book, Revelation, appeared near the end of the first century A.D. Thus, while the Old Testament may have taken about 1,000 years to write, the New Testament was written over only 50 years or so. Most of the letters of Paul and the epistle of James were probably written first. Matthew, Mark, and Luke wrote their gospels in the late 50s and in the 60s. Hebrews, 1 Peter, and 2 Peter may also have been written in the 60s. Very likely John wrote his gospel, his epistles, and Revelation later in the first century A.D.

## The New Testament Canon

The canon of the New Testament (the list of books considered to be Holy Scripture) was shaped by several factors: the desire to know about Jesus and His teachings, the need to fight heresy and persecution, and for use in worship services. Ultimately, as with the Old Testament, the books that became the New Testament impressed their readers as being different, special, and having the "ring of truth" about them. Most of the New Testament books are connected to an apostle as well (Mark is associated with Peter, Luke with Paul).[2]

The early Christian church did not "decide" what books were authoritative, but they did recognize the unique nature of the works that we know as the New Testament. In his Easter letter to his congregations in A.D. 367, Bishop Athanasius of Alexandria, Egypt, listed the 27 New Testament books as "divine" and called them "springs of salvation." In A.D. 397, at Carthage in North Africa, a church council met (with Augustine in attendance) and confirmed the canon of the New Testament. After that, very little significant discussion about which books belonged in the Bible took place until Reformation times. The Holy Spirit, who inspired the writers of Scripture, also guided the Christian church to identify which books are, in fact, part of the canon.

# Inspiration and Inerrancy

In the Bible God reveals Himself to people. He speaks honestly and bluntly about our problem (sin) and His solution (Christ crucified). He speaks the truth to us, both in the severity of the Law and the sweetness of the Gospel.

If the Bible is merely a human record of observations, meditations, and pious thoughts about God, we would expect errors of various sorts (historical, geographical, scientific, and the like). If it is truly God's Word, we would expect accuracy in both these smaller matters and the larger issues (such as the nature of God and the relationship between Him and us). We believe the original writings (called *autographs*) were inerrant, that is, contained no error of any sort.[3]

We also believe that Scripture is inspired, that is, that God is responsible for writing it. Inspiration differs from dictation, where God dictates the words of the Bible to a person who, as it were, is in a trance. But inspiration does not work this way. Read Luke 1:1–4 and answer the following:

1.   Is Luke an eyewitness of the events in his gospel?

2.   How did other writers get their information?

3.   How did Luke get his information?

4.   Where did Luke get the information in Luke 1 and 2?

5.   Does Luke claim to write a chronological account?

Luke is an eyewitness to some of the events in the second volume of his work (Acts),[4] but he is not present at the events he records in the gospel of Luke. Luke would have had a number of resources available to him, including eyewitnesses (such as Peter and other apostles) and the Jerusalem archives (e.g., the Apostolic Decree of Acts 15:22–29). Like other writers, Luke would have had to do research to get his information.

The material in Luke 1 and 2, so familiar to many Christians, is a good example of the kind of research Luke might have done. At the time Luke writes his gospel, almost everyone in those two chapters is dead. Jesus is, of course, alive, having ascended into heaven. Probably Luke's source is Mary herself. She would have known what she and the angel Gabriel discussed, what Elizabeth said when Mary visited her, and she alone would have known what she "pondered in her heart" when the shepherds came to the manger (Luke 2:19).

Although we cannot prove it, Luke could very well have interviewed Mary personally. If Luke wrote Luke and Acts during Paul's Roman imprisonment (A.D. 60–62), and if Mary gave birth to Jesus when she was in her early or middle teen years,[5] she would only have been in her early eighties at the time of the interview. Tradition locates her in her later years in Ephesus where the beloved disciple, John, conducted his ministry.[6] This would have been close enough to Rome for Luke to make the journey without seriously interrupting his time with Paul.[7]

In his introduction Luke claims to write an "orderly" account. This commonly means a chronological or sequential account of Jesus' life and public ministry and of how the Gospel got from Jerusalem to Rome. It doesn't mean that Luke didn't pull together certain teachings of Jesus under a specific topic or that every detail of his account is exactly chronological, but it does mean that Luke writes an accurate and coherent history of Jesus (gospel of Luke) and of the Gospel's spread (book of Acts).

Inspiration is not like dictation, but a more personal and subtle guidance of the writer to set down exactly the words God has chosen. The writer uses all his faculties and abilities in the process.

We have shown how Luke's process may have included an interview with Mary. However, it also is possible that Luke received his information from other sources. That possibility in no way undermines the fact that Luke wrote an inspired, inerrant account.

Peter addresses the subject of inspiration in 2 Peter 1:12–21. He reminds his readers of the transfiguration, which he personally witnessed (Matthew 17; Mark 9; Luke 9). There God's words confirmed the glory of Jesus. So also, Peter argues, the words of the Old Testament writers come from God, not from man. Peter includes New Testament writings as part of Holy Scripture in 2 Peter 3:15–16, where he classes Paul's writings with "the other Scriptures."

The point, then, is this: Jesus, the Word of God (John 1:1–18), is both human and divine. Scriptures, the written word of God, also have a divine side (origin, inspiration) and a human side (the authors and their world). Part of the adventure of Bible study is the investigation into the world of the authors of the books in the Bible. The things we learn equip us to understand more fully what we are reading.

# The Purpose of Scripture

The primary purpose of Scripture is to introduce us to Jesus Christ as our Savior and Lord (John 20:30–31). Read 2 Timothy 3:10–17 and answer the following:

1. What does it mean to say that Scripture is God-breathed?
2. Paul lists four functions of Scripture in verse 16. What are they?
3. What practical, day-to-day purpose does Scripture have?

*God-breathed* is a translation of *inspired*. This tells us that the source and essential characteristic of Scripture is that it comes from God and is God's own Word. Scripture *is* (not merely *contains*) the Word of God, as Jesus affirms in John 10:35, where He uses the two terms synonymously. The Bible is the source and standard for our teaching; it rebukes us (condemns us of our sin) and corrects us (guides us in the way that we should live). Confident of our salvation in Jesus Christ, we are thus completely equipped to live a life that honors God and shows others the way to salvation (see also Ephesians 2:8–10).

## Notes to Chapter 14

1 Scholars are divided on the dates of many of the New Testament books.

2 Connection to an apostle was not an absolute requirement for canonization, as is apparent from the fact that the book of Hebrews was accepted as authoritative even though it has no clear connection with an apostle.

3 This does not mean that mistakes have not been made in copying the autographs or in translating the original languages. We shall discuss this further in the next section.

4 In Acts 16:10 Luke switches from the third person ("they") to the first person ("we"), indicating that he joined Paul, Silas, and Timothy on the second missionary journey (about A.D. 50).

5 Jesus was most likely born in 5 or 6 B.C. An error in calculation by the monk who invented our system of counting years (Dionysius Exiguus) is responsible for the odd fact that Jesus was born several years B.C. (Before Christ).

6 Travelers to Ephesus today are often taken to the house that is said to have been Mary's house. Jesus had commended Mary into John's care at the cross (John 19:26).

7 Luke was a very faithful companion of Paul. At the end, shortly before Paul was executed, everyone had deserted him except Luke (2 Timothy 4:11).

## The Table of Dates

| | |
|---|---|
| 30 | Pentecost; Birthday of the New Testament Church |
| 32 | Death of Stephen and Conversion of St. Paul |
| 43 | Founding of Gentile Church at Antioch; Paul Summoned to Antioch by Barnabas |
| 44 | Death of James the Son of Zebedee |
| c. 45 | EPISTLE OF ST. JAMES |
| 46–48 | St. Paul's First Missionary Journey |
| 48 | EPISTLE TO THE GALATIANS |
| 49 | Apostolic Council |
| 49–51 | St. Paul's Second Missionary Journey |
| 50 (early) | 1 THESSALONIANS |
| 50 (summer) | 2 THESSALONIANS |
| 52–56 | St. Paul's Third Missionary Journey |
| 55 (spring) | 1 CORINTHIANS |
| 55 (summer or fall) | 2 CORINTHIANS |
| 56 (early) | ROMANS |
| 56–58 | St. Paul's Caesarean Imprisonment |
| 58–59 | St. Paul's Voyage to Rome |
| 59–61 | St. Paul's Roman Imprisonment |
| 59–61 | COLOSSIANS, PHILEMON, EPHESIANS, PHILIPPIANS (The Captivity Letters) |
| 50–70 | GOSPEL ACCORDING TO ST. MATTHEW |
| c. 60 | GOSPEL ACCORDING TO ST. MARK |
| 62–63 | 1 TIMOTHY |
| 63 | TITUS |
| 64 | Fire in Rome. Neronian Persecution |
| 65–67 | 2 TIMOTHY |
| 61–62 | 1 PETER |
| 62 (?) | 2 PETER |
| 65–69 | GOSPEL ACCORDING TO ST. LUKE. THE BOOK OF ACTS |
| 60–70 | JUDE |
| 56–70 | HEBREWS |
| 70 | Fall of Jerusalem |
| 90–100 | GOSPEL ACCORDING TO ST. JOHN. 1, 2, 3 JOHN |
| 95 | REVELATION OF ST. JOHN |

# English Translations and Paraphrases

One of the most important accomplishments of Martin Luther, the 16th-century German reformer, was that he translated the Bible from the original languages into the common language of his day. By doing so, he empowered people to read the Bible for themselves. Only one English translation, the King James Version (KJV; produced in 1611) has come close to the popularity of Luther's German Bible. However, the KJV was not the first English translation.

John Wycliffe produced an English translation of the official Roman Catholic Bible, the Latin Vulgate,[1] in the 14th century. Not long after that, the church banned all translations. It became a capital crime to translate the Bible from its original Hebrew or Greek, or to translate the Latin Vulgate, into a modern language. This did not stop translation efforts. William Tyndale, the "Father of the English Bible," translated the New Testament and parts of the Old Testament before he was arrested and executed in 1536. A number of other English translations followed, but all were overshadowed by the translation ordered by King James, completed in 1611.

A team of 54 translators worked for seven years to produce what would become the most popular English Bible of all time. It underwent a number of revisions over the following decades, but remained largely the Bible that had been presented to King James.

The appearance of so many modern translations has confused people, particularly those who had come to love the KJV. When someone goes into a Christian bookstore to buy a Bible, the variety of choices can be intimidating. Some translations are better than others, so how do we pick the "right" one? Paraphrases differ from translations, but they are easier to read. Should we buy a paraphrase or a translation? And finally, why are there so many translations and paraphrases?

## Chart of Bible Translations with Abbreviations

| | |
|---|---|
| King James Version/New King James Version | KJV/NKJV |
| Revised Standard Version/New Revised Standard Version | RSV/NRSV |
| New American Standard Bible | NASB |
| New International Version | NIV |
| Today's English Version/Contemporary English Version | TEV/CEV |
| New Century Version | NCV |
| The Living Bible/New Living Translation | LB/NLT |
| Jerusalm Bible | JB |
| Revised English Bible | REB |

# Translation

The words in one language don't "line up" exactly with the words in another language. That is to say, every word has the possibility of communicating one or more meanings. The range of meanings a word can communicate are not identical from one language to the next.

As an example, let's look at the Greek word *pneuma*. We get our English words *pneumonia* and *pneumatic* from this word. Depending on context, *pneuma* can be accurately translated into English as *spirit* or as *breath* or as *wind* or even as a reference to the Holy Spirit. In the right context, it can refer to the whole self of a person (as in Mary's Magnificat, Luke 1:47).[2] No English word has the capacity to mean all these different things, so the translator must make many difficult choices.

Every translation reflects these choices. As a result, translations differ from one another. An additional problem occurs when English itself changes over a period of time. Take Psalm 7:9 as an example. In the last line of that verse, the King James reads

"For the righteous God trieth the hearts and reins."

The English language no longer uses *reins* in the way that the King James translators meant it. There the word *reins* referred to the kidneys. Still, it is not much of an improvement to translate it "For the righteous God trieth the hearts and kidneys." The meaning of the psalmist doesn't become clear to us until we realize that *trieth* means *put to the test,* that *heart* refers to the organ of thought·and will (that is, the mind), and that kidneys were thought to be the seat of emotion (what we today would call the heart). Here the New Revised Standard Version (NRSV) has a better translation, "You who test the minds and hearts, O righteous God."

The translator has to decide whether to use the English word that anatomically translates the Hebrew or the English word that functionally translates the Hebrew. That is to say, shall the translator give us a "literal" translation or a "dynamic" translation? Most translations try to stay as literal as possible, while most paraphrases are unabashedly dynamic.

One ancient rabbi is reported to have said that "a man who claims to make a literal translation is a liar and he who makes a paraphrase should be executed." Every translation reflects the philosophy, beliefs, and theological orientation of the translator. The best translations minimize this, but the background of the translator is always present.

As if all this were not enough, translators currently struggle with yet another issue: should the translation be gender-neutral or should it reflect the gender bias of the original languages? For example, Paul uses the phrase "sons of God" in Romans 8:14 and 8:19 and Galatians 3:26 to refer to all believers, men and women. Should the translator let stand the phrase "sons of God" or should it be changed to "children of God"? By extension, Jesus teaches us to pray to the "Father" (Matthew 6:9; Luke 11:2). Should this be changed to "parent"? Jesus would then become the "child" of the heavenly "parent" instead of Son of the Father. We can see how questions of translation often involve much larger questions of theology.

# Current English Bibles

"Of making many books there is no end, and much study is a weariness of the flesh" (Ecclesiastes 12:12). What Solomon said about books in the 10th century B.C. is still true today, including different versions of the Bible. We won't discuss every translation available but will concentrate on four popular versions: King James/New King James, Revised Standard/New Revised Standard, New American Standard/New American Standard Updated, and the New International Version.

## The King James Version/New King James Version

As noted earlier, this translation goes back to the early 17th century. The richness of language, the beauty of its poetical sections, and the reliability and consistency of translation continue to make it an excellent choice for the modern Bible reader. Two weaknesses, however, should be noted.

The original language texts upon which the KJV was based were produced very late. Much earlier copies of the Hebrew and Greek manuscripts have been found since the KJV translators did their work. The three best-known New Testament examples are Mark 16:9–20 (the ending of Mark), John 7:53–8:11 (the story of the woman caught in the act of adultery), and 1 John 5:7–8 (technically known as the *Johanine Comma*). Ancient manuscripts discovered in the last century or so have indicated that these three sections were not part of the original writing (the *autograph*). A number of other, much smaller differences exist between the oldest and best manuscripts of the Bible and the Hebrew and Greek texts that the KJV translators had in their day.

Secondly, the English language has changed somewhat since the KJV was prepared in 1611. For example, we no longer use the same second-person pronouns or certain verb forms. ("Thou gavest me the book" is now "You gave me the book.") Words have altered meaning as well. Instead of "Suffer the little children," we would say, "Permit the little children" (Matthew 19:14). Likewise, it makes little sense today to ask if the living will "prevent" the dead at the second coming of Jesus

(1 Thessalonians 4:15). *Prevent*, from the Latin *pre venio* ("I come before"), denoted an advantage. Will the living precede the dead at the resurrection? That is, will the living have an advantage over the dead when Jesus returns? Paul answers no, but modern readers of the KJV might have a hard time understanding the question.

The New King James Version, introduced in 1982, offers a new translation of the Greek and Hebrew originals along the lines of the KJV but without the anachronisms of the 17th century. Its biggest weakness is that, like the KJV, it does not take into account recent manuscript discoveries.

## The Revised Standard Version/ New Revised Standard Version

The Revised Standard Version first appeared as a New Testament (1946) and then with the Old Testament (1951). It was a new translation from the Hebrew and Greek and took into account the manuscript discoveries up to that point.

The theological orientation of the translators may be seen in places where word choice or punctuation is critical. For example, in Isaiah 7:14 the prophet predicts that a virgin will give birth to a child whose name will be Immanuel. Matthew believes this is fulfilled when Mary, a virgin, gives birth to Jesus (Matthew 1:23). The Hebrew word translated *virgin* in the KJV is translated *young woman* in the RSV. In making this choice, was the RSV committee reluctant to support a traditional understanding of Christ?

Some have criticized the RSV punctuation in Romans 9:5. The original manuscripts contained no punctuation. Editors and translators determined where to place the punctuation marks. The RSV reads, "To [the Israelites] belong the patriarchs, and of their race, according to the flesh, is the Christ. God who is over all be blessed for ever. Amen." The period after *Christ* avoided calling Jesus *God* in this verse.

The NRSV (1989) has changed this, altering the period to a comma, so that it now reads "to them belong the patriarchs, and from them, according to the flesh, comes the Messiah, who is over all, God blessed forever. Amen." The NRSV calls Jesus God at this point. The NRSV has gained respect and acceptance although some criticize it for using gender-neutral terminology ("inclusive language") in many places.

## The New American Standard/
## New American Standard Updated

The New American Standard Bible (NASB) became available in 1971. It is a conservative translation that tries to maintain the original verb tenses (and other elements of speech) in its translation. The NASB lends itself very well to Bible study. However, when read aloud, it often sounds a bit "wooden." It was updated in 1995 and is more fluid than its predecessor, conforming more to American syntax and grammar.

## The New International Version

Published first in 1978, the New International Version (NIV) has become somewhat of a standard in many churches and homes. It is much easier to read aloud and reasonably conservative as a translation. It is not without its criticisms, however. Some have suggested it lacks the beauty and richness of the KJV, but is admittedly easier to understand. As with all translations, it could be improved at places.[3]

# Paraphrases

A paraphrase is a very dynamic rendering of the Bible. Sometimes the paraphrase starts by using the Greek and Hebrew and sometimes not.

## Today's English Version/Contemporary English Version

*Good News: Today's English Version (TEV),* which came out in 1976, is a very popular paraphrase. It was produced by the American Bible Society with the intent that it would be readable by the vast majority of

English speakers. Language was to be kept "natural, clear, simple, and unambiguous."

Perhaps the biggest weakness of the TEV is that it tends to make the rich language of Scripture so simple as to sound flat. For example, Jesus uses the word *blessed* in the Beatitudes (Matthew 5:1–12). The TEV renders that word as *happy*. "Happy are the meek" does not convey the point Jesus makes: the meek here are blessed because in the future they will inherit the kingdom of God, the new heaven and new earth, which follows the resurrection. Jesus promises more to the meek than happiness usually associated with the word *happy* today. He says that those who do not insist upon their own way but put faith in Jesus Christ will find themselves inheriting the world. Some who follow Jesus' directions will end up like He did, without even a place to lay their heads (Matthew 8:20). God's gracious favor (blessedness) on the believer reaches its culmination in the next age. TEV's *happy* can turn the rich and complex *blessed* into the flat and misleading *happy*.

In 1995 the American Bible Society published the Contemporary English Version (CEV) to replace the TEV. In this translation the beatitude about the meek (Matthew 5:5) reads, "God blesses those people who are humble. The earth will belong to them!" Like the NRSV, the CEV uses gender-neutral terminology in many places.

## The Living Bible

Kenneth Taylor's *The Living Bible* (LB) has become very popular. It is a retelling of the biblical story based on the King James Version, with the goal that it be simple and understandable. It is indeed simple and understandable, but it often departs greatly from the biblical text. Two examples will illustrate the point.

In 1 Corinthians 16:24 Paul writes, "My love *be* with all of you in Christ Jesus." This is a fairly literal translation. It supplies the verb *be*, since the original does not explicitly state the verb.[4] The *Living Bible* reads, "My love to all of you, for we all belong to Christ Jesus. Sincerely, Paul." The *LB* rendition is easy to read and understand, but it is not what God inspired Paul to write.

A more significant variation occurs at Revelation 13:18. In this famous "666" passage two beasts, one from the sea and one from the land, appear to help Satan fight Christians. The first beast (13:1–10) represents anti-Christian government. The second beast represents anti-Christian religion. Both are symbols of patterns that will occur throughout the New Testament age. Faced with governmental persecution, the Christian needs endurance and faith (13:10b). Faced with deceptive religions, the Christian needs wisdom from God (13:18). A fairly literal translation of 13:18 reads, "Here is *the need for* wisdom. The one having a mind, let him calculate the number of the beast, for it is man's number, and his number is six hundred sixty-six."

Two big questions present themselves. What does the number 666 represent, and does it refer to one man or to more than one man? Strictly speaking, one can translate *man's* as *a man's,* although this is very unlikely. Had John meant one specific man, he could have said *a certain man* or *one man.* It is far more likely that John intends us to understand that 666 (a symbolic number that refers to man's failed efforts to become God) applies to the whole human race and specifically to false teachers.[5]

Alternative ways of interpreting 666 include *gematria* (counting the numerical value of the letters in a name) and *triangulation* (1-8 = 36, 1-36 = 666, therefore the important number is 8). A good translation or paraphrase will translate this verse in such a way as to let you, the reader, make the interpretation. A bad translation will take all options away from the reader, leaving you with only the translator's opinion. Some translations render *man's number* (NIV), *number of a person* (NRSV), and *number of a man* (NKJV). Here the NIV is the best translation, because it lets the English reader wrestle with the text. The *LB* takes all choice away and misleads the reader with Kenneth Taylor's own millenialist theology: "Here is a puzzle that calls for careful thought to solve it. Let those who are able, interpret this code: the numerical values of the letters in his name add to 666!"

Paraphrases in general, and *The Living Bible* in particular, are best when you want to read long sections of the Bible in a short time. They tend not to be very good for verse-by-verse Bible study, because so much of the translator's opinion is included in the transmission process from the original language text to the English. A recent revision of this paraphrase, now called *The New Living Translation,* attempts to address the weaknesses of the original *Living Bible.*

# Choosing the Right Bible

Perhaps the place to start is to ask the question, "What do I want to do with my Bible?" If I want to read the entire Bible in 12 months, perhaps a good paraphrase is best. If I need to prepare a Sunday school lesson, then maybe I should buy a study Bible. If you do buy a study Bible, remember that the notes are not God's Word—only the text itself is. Therefore one is wise to purchase a reliable study Bible, such as the *Concordia Self-Study Bible.*

You may also want to ask a friend or someone at church who teaches Bible classes what they would recommend. A well-informed clerk at a Christian bookstore also could help you. Don't be afraid to look through several editions to see which one offers you the extras that you want.

When examining a Bible, check passages that reveal the translator's orientation. We have already noted Isaiah 7:14, Matthew 5:5, Romans 9:5, and Revelation 13:18. Also take time to read the introduction. Those pages that precede Genesis 1 might tell you all you need to learn about a particular Bible. Last, but certainly not least, pray about your choice. Also do so each time you start your Bible study. Ask the Holy Spirit to guide you. Why not also ask Him to help you choose the best one for you? After all, who knows a book better than its author?

# Notes to Chapter 15

1  In the fourth century A.D. Jerome translated the Hebrew and Greek manuscripts into Latin, the common language ("vulgar tongue") of his day. The Roman Catholic Church adopted this as its official Bible.

2  Hebrew has no reflexive pronoun. You cannot say myself in Hebrew. Instead, you would say my soul or my spirit.

3  Certainly the title for God could be improved. The NIV renders Adonai Yahweh as "Sovereign LORD" (e.g., Genesis 15:2). Perhaps the names of God could simply be transliterated (as above) with an introductory note on their meaning.

4  This is quite common in Greek texts and is called ellipsis. The reader is expected to fill in the verb.

5  This is confirmed by practical experience. Many religious teachers, especially in the New Age movement, proclaim that we are "gods."

# Ancient Books and Writings Outside the Bible

Does the Bible contain all the books written during ancient times? Certainly not! Only a few of the works produced by ancient authors appear in the Bible. In fact, a number of epistles and gospels claimed to have been written by apostles were never considered Scripture. Not even all the letters written by New Testament authors were preserved. We have evidence for at least three letters of Paul that have not survived.[1] The modern Bible student may well ask what kinds of literature existed during Bible times and what impact, if any, does that literature have on Bible study?

In this section we will look at three groups of books: the Dead Sea Scrolls, the Nag Hammadi Library, and Old Testament apocrypha and pseudepigrapha.

## The Dead Sea Scrolls

Of all the literature outside of the Bible in ancient times, the Dead Sea Scrolls are probably the most well known. In 1947 an Arab youth, a shepherd looking for his goats, accidentally discovered some ancient manuscripts preserved in sealed jars and hidden in a cave near the Dead Sea. Over the next 10 years archaeologists found a number of other manuscripts in other caves. Eleven relatively complete scrolls were eventually discovered, along with thousands of fragments of other scrolls, some as small as a fingernail.

The scrolls and scroll fragments fall into three categories: books of the Old Testament,[2] commentaries on the Old Testament,[3] and sectarian writings.[4] These were apparently preserved by a group of religious separatists who were eradicated by the Romans in A.D. 70. Josephus, an ancient historian, mentions a group of separatists living in this area. He called them Essenes. Many scholars think the Dead Sea Scrolls belonged to these people.

The most immediate and obvious benefit from these scrolls is that we have verified the reliability of the Hebrew Scriptures. About 95 percent of the Bible texts at Qumran (the name for the place where the scrolls were found) conform to the type of Hebrew text preserved in the Hebrew text as it was passed down to us.[5]

These scrolls, especially the documents originating with the Essene sect, made a second contribution. They provide a window into one of the many diverse groups that made up Judaism in the first century A.D. We see a group of people who, like John the Baptist, rejected the more mainstream Judaism of the Pharisees and Sadducees. In fact, shortly after the discovery of the Dead Sea Scrolls some people thought John the Baptist might have spent some time in the Qumran community, but those suggestions have largely fallen out of favor among scholars. The people who lived at Qumran believed themselves to be the true Israel. They looked for the arrival of the Messianic age and the destruction of their enemies in Jerusalem. The Romans, however, destroyed them.

Have the Dead Sea Scrolls changed the Bible at all? Not really. In a few places, modern translations of the Old Testament (especially the NRSV) have taken into account the Hebrew Scriptures found at Qumran. Aside from a few small alterations in the Old Testament, the Dead Sea Scrolls have not challenged the text of the Bible. These small alterations have not changed any doctrines.

One can find many inexpensive books on the Dead Sea Scrolls. These three provide a sample:

Geza Vermes. *The Dead Sea Scrolls*. London: Penguin Books, 1987.

Hershel Shanks, ed. *Understanding the Dead Sea Scrolls: A Reader from the "Biblical Archaeology Review."* New York: Random House, 1992.

Hershel Shanks, James C. Vanderkam, P. Kyle McCarter, Jr., and James A. Sanders. *The Dead Sea Scrolls After Forty Years.* Washington, D.C.: Biblical Archaeology Society, 1992.

# The Nag Hammadi Library

Like the Dead Sea Scrolls, the Nag Hammadi Library was an accidental discovery. Stored in a clay jar,[6] 13 documents from as early as the third and fourth centuries A.D. were discovered in Egypt. Their discovery turned out to be much more dramatic than that of the Dead Sea Scrolls, involving intrigue, theft, murder, and even cannibalism.[7]

Writers from heretical Christian sects apparently wrote the Nag Hammadi documents. The writings reflect a type of false teaching broadly known as *gnosticism*. Gnosticism generally emphasized secret knowledge, denied the incarnation of Christ as well as the crucifixion, and had a strong interest in angels. (Gnosticism and New Age philosophy have much in common, particularly cosmic dualism, angelology, and a rejection of the cross of Christ.) The best known of these works is the Gospel of Thomas. At the end of this collection of supposed sayings of Jesus, we read

> Simon Peter said to them: let Mary go away from us, for women
> are not worthy of life. Jesus said: Lo, I shall lead her, so that I may
> make her a male, and that she too may become a living spirit
> (pneuma), resembling you males. For every woman who makes
> herself a male will enter the kingdom of heaven.[8]

We easily recognize that this teaching stands in opposition to the clear teaching of the Bible. Holy Scripture teaches that women are created in the image of God (Genesis 1:26–27), are equally part of God's family of believers (Galatians 3:26–29), and are fellow heirs of the kingdom of God (1 Peter 3:7).

Does the Nag Hammadi Library affect our faith? No, it has no impact on the Bible or on our Christian beliefs. It does show us that early Christianity faced challenges other than persecution and the pressure of pagan religions. Christians also had to fight against heretical movements that claimed Jesus as their founder, too.

The Nag Hammadi Library contains a number of other works that are produced under the title "Gospel" or under the name of an apostle. While these writings are interesting, they don't really have any direct relationship to the New Testament. The following books provide additional information about the Nag Hammadi Library:

Willis Barnstone, ed. *The Other Bible: Ancient Alternative Scriptures.* San Francisco: Harper, 1984.

Charles W. Hedrick and Robert Hodgson, Jr. *Nag Hammadi, Gnosticism, and Early Christianity.* Peabody: Hendrickson Publishers, 1986.

John McRay. *Archaeology & The New Testament.* Grand Rapids: Baker Book House, 1991.

Elaine Pagels. *The Gnostic Gospels.* New York: Random House, 1979.

Wilhelm Schneemelcher, ed. *New Testament Apocrypha.* Cambridge: James Clarke & Co., 1991.

# Old Testament Apocrypha and Pseudepigrapha

We also need to distinguish between those books that are considered part of Scripture and those that are non-biblical. If you look at a Roman Catholic Bible, you will see that it has several more books in the Old Testament than does a Protestant Bible. These books are Tobit, Judith, Additions to the Book of Esther, Wisdom of Solomon, Ecclesiasticus (also known as the Wisdom of Jesus ben Sirach), Baruch, the Letter of Jeremiah (or Baruch 6), Additions to the Book of Daniel (the Prayer of Azariah and the Son of the Three Young Men, Susanna, Bel and the Dragon), and 1 and 2 Maccabees.

The Roman Catholic, Greek Orthodox, and Russian Orthodox Churches accept these as Deuterocanonical Scripture ("Second Canon"). Most Protestants do not regard these as part of the Bible, because they were never part of the Hebrew Scriptures. However, the Greek translation of the Old Testament (the Septuagint) contained these books. Since Jerome included these books in his Latin Vulgate, and since the Vulgate is the official Bible of the Roman Catholic Church, they were considered Scripture. Protestants called these works *apocrypha*, but the Roman Catholic Church designates them as Deuterocanonical. They are worth reading—particularly 1 and 2 Maccabbees, which traces the history of the Jewish people in the first and second centuries before Christ.

A second category of extra-biblical books is designated *pseudepigrapha*. These writings were produced throughout the intertestamental period (400 B.C. to the birth of Christ) and into the New Testament age. The term *pseudepigrapha* is a transliteration of a Greek work that denotes writings with false superscriptions, that is, books that claim to be written by famous people of the past (e.g., Moses, Enoch, the Twelve Patriarchs). James Charlesworth has collected 52 writings that have these five elements in common:

1. The writings have a Jewish or Christian origin.[9]
2. They are attributed to the great figures of Jewish history.
3. They claim to be a communication from God.
4. They reflect Old Testament narratives.
5. They were composed sometime between 200 B.C. and A.D. 200.

Some of these books are fairly sober (e.g., the Testament of the Twelve Patriarchs), while others are more like Revelation (1 Enoch). Some "fill in the gaps" in the Old Testament, adding stories about minor characters (like Jannes and Jambres, the two magicians who battled Moses in Pharaoh's court). Others reflect more current history (like the Letter of

Aristeas, which tells how the Septuagint [the Greek translation of the Hebrew Scriptures] was made).

How do these works help us study the Bible? First, they give us added insight into the world in which Jesus conducted his earthly ministry. As a result of reading some of these books we can better appreciate the diversity of thought and the differences between the divisions within first-century Judaism.

Second, we get a clearer picture of the Messianic expectations people held at the time of Christ. For example, in the Psalms of Solomon (written in the first century B.C.) we read of the coming Messiah and the destruction that he will bring to Gentiles and to sinners in general (Psalms of Solomon 17:21–25). This work reveals the expectation that when Messiah came, he would set up a glorious kingdom of wealth and power, like his ancestor David.

Some of the apostles may have had this in mind when they left their homes and families and careers to follow Jesus. They expected a really big payday when Jesus came into His own. This is obvious from the times the disciples argued among themselves as to who was the greatest. The request of James and John to sit on Jesus' right and left in His glorious kingdom (Mark 10:35–37) indicates that they looked for an earthly kingdom. Perhaps Peter speaks for the entire band when he asks Jesus what payment they will receive for following Jesus (Matthew 19:27). They expected to receive this payment once Jesus set up the kind of kingdom anticipated in many of the pseudepigrapha.

## Summary and Conclusions

The Dead Sea Scrolls and other extra-canonical books do not challenge our confidence in the Holy Scriptures. They provide background information for us that helps us to study the Bible with understanding as we learn more about the ancient world. By reading these books we may even appreciate the Bible more than before!

Scripture is straightforward, honest about our sin, and crystal clear about our Savior, Jesus Christ. The adventure of Bible study begins anew each day. Along the way we may take time to pick up some history or read books that people wrote during the same centuries the Bible was being written. We come to know God's Word better as we grow in our ability to understand what He says and apply it to our lives. May God bless you as you continue to read the word, pray for the Spirit's guidance, and share it with others!

## Notes to Chapter 16

1   Paul refers to a previous letter to the Corinthians, now lost, in 1 Corinthians 5:9–13. He mentions a "severe letter" to Corinth, written between First and Second Corinthians, in 2 Corinthians 2:3–9 and 7:8–12. That letter has not been found. Paul also commends to the Colossians the letter he wrote to the Laodiceans, but we do not have such a letter today.

2   About one fourth of the texts are biblical texts, representing every book of the Old Testament except Esther. It may be significant that Esther is the only Hebrew Scripture that does not mention God.

3   These include commentaries as well as meditations on the Bible, such as hymns and psalms.

4   Some of these are religious, some are not. One of them, the Copper Scroll, seems to be a treasure map!

5   The Hebrew text that was formerly the oldest copy of the Old Testament is known as the "Leningrad Codex" (a codex is a type of book) dating to approximately A.D. 1000.

6   Jeremiah also stored important documents in a clay jar in the sixth century B.C. (Jeremiah 32:14).

7   Both McRay's book and Pagel's volume tell the story of their discovery.

8   Logion 118, taken from the *Synopsis Quattuor Evangeliorum* (Stuttgart: Wüerttembergische Bibelanstalt, 1967), 8th edition, page 530.

9   In *The Old Testament Pseudepigrapha* (Garden City, N.Y.: Doubleday, 1985), James Charlesworth notes that the lone exception is Ahiqar.